BASIC JUDAISM FOR YOUNG PEOPLE: **GOD**

BASIC JUDAISM FOR YOUNG PEOPLE

VOLUME THREE

NAOMI PASACHOFF, PH.D.

BEHRMAN HOUSE, INC., PUBLISHERS

In loving memory of Diana J. Reisman, ז״ל *, and of Samuel S. Pasachoff,* ז״ל

Designer: Betty Binns Graphics/Martin Lubin
Artists: Ronald F. Hall, Winslow Pinney Pells, and Jody Wheeler
Project Editor: Geoffrey Horn

The editor and publisher gratefully acknowledge the cooperation of the following sources of photographs for this book:

Bill Aron, 14, 33, 55, 64, 90, 141; Bruno Barbey/Magnum, 16; Bettmann Archive, 76, 142–43; FourByFive, 4, 12–13, 32, 39, 42, 53, 80, 85, 104–05, 116, 118–19, 120, 132; Brian Furner/Photo Researchers, 44; Louis Goldman/Photo Researchers, 97; Hebrew Union College-Skirball Museum, 40, 41, 69, 99, 113; Paolo Koch/Photo Researchers, 24; Roger Malloch/Magnum, 94; Tom McHugh/Photo Researchers, 135; Chuck Muhlstock/Black Star, 62; Jay Pasachoff, 2; Photo Researchers, 125; Earl Roberge/Photo Researchers, 108; Blair Seitz/Photo Researchers, 133, 140; Katrina Thomas/Photo Researchers, 30; Wide World, 46–47.

Library of Congress Cataloging-in-Publication Data
(Revised for vol. 3)

Pasachoff, Naomi E.
   Basic Judaism for young people.
   "Artists: Marlies Merk Najaka and Jody Wheeler"—v. 1, p. iv;
   "Artists: Tony Chen and Jody Wheeler"—v. 2, p. iv;
   "Artists: Ronald F. Hall, Winslow Pinney Pels, and Jody Wheeler"—v. 3, p. iv.
   Includes indexes.
   Contents: v. 1. Israel—v. 2. Torah—v. 3. God.
   1. Judaism—Juvenile literature. 2. Judaism—Dictionaries. I. Najaka, Marlies, ill. II. Wheeler, Jody, ill. III. Chen, Tony, ill. IV. Hall, Ronald, ill. V. Pels, Winslow, ill. VI. Title.
BM573.P37   1986   296   86-1214
ISBN 0-87441-425-3 (v. 3)

Front cover: Illustrations by Ronald F. Hall (animals, garden, sea with ark) and Winslow Pinney Pels (lame man and blind man). Photographs courtesy of Bill Aron (Havdalah) and FourByFive (galaxy, family walk).
Back cover: Roger Malloch/Magnum.

BASIC JUDAISM FOR YOUNG PEOPLE

VOLUME THREE

NAOMI PASACHOFF, PH.D.

BEHRMAN HOUSE, INC., PUBLISHERS

In loving memory of Diana J. Reisman, ז״ל*,
and of Samuel S. Pasachoff,* ז״ל

Copyright © 1987 by Naomi Pasachoff

Designer: Betty Binns Graphics/Martin Lubin
Artists: Ronald F. Hall, Winslow Pinney Pells, and Jody Wheeler
Project Editor: Geoffrey Horn

*The editor and publisher gratefully acknowledge the cooperation of the
following sources of photographs for this book:*

Bill Aron, 14, 33, 55, 64, 90, 141; Bruno Barbey/Magnum, 16; Bettmann Archive, 76,
142–43; FourByFive, 4, 12–13, 32, 39, 42, 53, 80, 85, 104–05, 116, 118–19, 120, 132;
Brian Furner/Photo Researchers, 44; Louis Goldman/Photo Researchers, 97;
Hebrew Union College-Skirball Museum, 40, 41, 69, 99, 113; Paolo Koch/Photo
Researchers, 24; Roger Malloch/Magnum, 94; Tom McHugh/Photo Researchers,
135; Chuck Muhlstock/Black Star, 62; Jay Pasachoff, 2; Photo Researchers, 125; Earl
Roberge/Photo Researchers, 108; Blair Seitz/Photo Researchers, 133, 140; Katrina
Thomas/Photo Researchers, 30; Wide World, 46–47.

Library of Congress Cataloging-in-Publication Data
(Revised for vol. 3)

Pasachoff, Naomi E.
    Basic Judaism for young people.

    "Artists: Marlies Merk Najaka and Jody Wheeler"—v. 1, p. iv;
    "Artists: Tony Chen and Jody Wheeler"—v. 2, p. iv;
    "Artists: Ronald F. Hall, Winslow Pinney Pels, and Jody Wheeler"—v. 3,
p. iv.
    Includes indexes.
    Contents: v. 1. Israel—v. 2. Torah—v. 3. God.
    1. Judaism—Juvenile literature. 2. Judaism—Dictionaries. I. Najaka,
Marlies, ill. II. Wheeler, Jody, ill. III. Chen, Tony, ill. IV. Hall, Ronald, ill. V.
Pels, Winslow, ill. VI. Title.
BM573.P37   1986   296   86-1214
ISBN 0-87441-425-3 (v. 3)

Front cover: Illustrations by Ronald F. Hall (animals, garden, sea with
ark) and Winslow Pinney Pels (lame man and blind man). Photographs
courtesy of Bill Aron (Havdalah) and FourByFive (galaxy, family walk).
Back cover: Roger Malloch/Magnum.

CONTENTS

FOREWORD
TO THE TEACHER

Some Jews contend that Judaism is not concerned with theology, as are other religious traditions. These people hold that our tradition is one of deed, not creed; action, not intention; practice, not theory. Many people dismiss not only Jewish theology but also Jewish belief. What is important in Judaism, they insist, is what is felt "in the heart" or what is accomplished through actions. To justify this separation of thought and feeling, they tell the story of the rabbi's disciple who complained that he could not pray because he had a severe headache. "What does the head have to do with the heart?" the rabbi is reported to have answered.

We would argue, on the contrary, that the head and the heart have much in common. Our children are shown how to don the Tefillin. They are properly taught that binding the head and arm phylacteries signifies the interdependence of head, heart, and hand in a ritual act of oneness. Belonging, behaving, and believing sustain each other.

This third volume of Naomi Pasachoff's *Basic Judaism for Young People* deals with God, a subject we have difficulty teaching about in our religious schools. My own experience in ḥeder was that whenever we asked questions about God, the teacher was forever promising "Later, later." But later never came.

Some people insist that children are too young to deal with philosophical issues: the existence and nature of God, the purpose of prayer, the role of miracles in the Bible. Others rationalize avoidance of "God-talk" by contending that "Jews have no dogmas." Of this claim, Solomon Schechter observed that the only dogma Jews hold is that they have no dogmas.

We who teach Bible and Siddur, the sacred texts of our curriculum, know that children do ask theological questions. The questions children ask about life and death, fate and free will, good and evil, punishment and reward, cannot be denied a central place in the Jewish curriculum. Age-appropriate discussion is important because, in its absence, the vacuum that develops is filled by uninformed and superstitious "street theology."

We must engage the child's religious curiosity respectfully and undogmatically. A rabbinic text ponders how one God could be revealed individually to 600,000 Jews at the foot of Mount Sinai. God is one, and yet He appears to each listener differently. R. Levi suggested: God appeared to them like a mirror, in which many faces can be reflected. So when God spoke to the Children of Israel, each person thought that God spoke to him or her directly. That is why the Torah (Exodus 20:2) speaks in the singular: אָנֹכִי יְהֹוָה אֱלֹהֶיךָ . Another sage, R. Yose bar Ḥanina, said that when God spoke to the Children of Israel, each one heard according to his or her own power. Just as the manna tasted different to each, so the divine voice sounded different.

Judaism has many different ways of thinking about the nature of God and about God's role in history. Shammai is not Hillel, Akiba is not Ishmael ben Elisha, and Mordecai Kaplan is not Martin Buber. This pluralistic heritage makes an important contribution to our teaching. Awareness of such a rich diversity of approaches ought to encourage you as a teacher to share your own religious experiences with your students, and should lead your students to think creatively about the place of God in their own lives.

The lure of literalism reduces Bible and liturgy to its most limited sense. In our text we have tried to encourage students to understand the value of Midrashic imagination in reading sacred materials. Our sages struggled against the anthropomorphism that took God's outstretched arm as an arm of flesh and blood. The rabbis of the Talmud warned that the Torah was written in the language of people. They sought to convey the idea that God did not have physical features. Students can and should be taught to distinguish metaphor, simile, allegory, and myth from flat statements of fact.

The deepest questions in life are not subject to simple true-or-false answers. To questions about the reality or truth of events in the Bible, the teacher may want to explore the idea that there are many levels of reality and truth. Are love, compassion, and kindness real? Can poetry, art, and music be true?

There are many ways to frame questions about God. For example, if we ask *where* God is, we direct attention to God as a being occupying place or space. But if we ask *when* God is, we focus a student's attention on time and event, on the Jewish past, present, and future. The *Fragestellung* — the way the question is posed — opens the child to alternative ways of thinking about God.

Most important for all of us who teach Judaism is to keep open the imagination of our students and to encourage the speculations of their wondering minds and hearts. In theological matters, good teaching is open-ended. The conclusion of each discussion should open the way to further thinking and feeling.

RABBI HAROLD M. SCHULWEIS

PREFACE
TO THE STUDENT

People have always thought about God. In times of sadness or joy, anger or love, illness or health, poverty or plenty, people have used the idea of God to express deep feelings beyond the reach of everyday language. When they experienced something beautiful, they wrote soaring hymns of praise to God; when they experienced something painful or ugly, they wrote dirges, laments, or, in modern times, the blues.

We rely on the idea of God not only to express extremes of emotion but also to express our feelings about our own place in the universe. At times God seems to be the farthest object outside our reach, as impossibly distant as the most remote star. At other times God seems to be the most inward and intensely private part of our selves.

All these contrasts, and many others, are suggested by our textbook, the third and final volume of *Basic Judaism for Young People*. Now that you are not quite so young any more, you can start thinking about God in new ways. Welcome, then, to the subject that crowns the study of Jewish life.

RABBI WILLIAM CUTTER

The Alef-Bet אָלֶף בֵּית

ENGLISH SOUND	ENGLISH NAME	NUMBER VALUE	HEBREW NAME	LETTER
—	alef	1	אָלֶף	א
b	bet	2	בֵּית	בּ
v	vet		בֵית	ב
g	gimmel	3	גִּמֶל	ג
d	dalet	4	דָּלֶת	ד
h	hay	5	הֵא	ה
v	vav	6	וָו	ו
z	zayin	7	זַיִן	ז
ḥ	ḥet	8	חֵית	ח
t	tet	9	טֵית	ט
y	yod	10	יוֹד	י
k	kaf	20	כַּף	כּ
ḥ	chaf		כַף	כ
ḥ	final chaf		כַף סוֹפִית	ך
l	lamed	30	לָמֶד	ל
m	mem	40	מֵם	מ
m	final mem		מֵם סוֹפִית	ם
n	nun	50	נוּן	נ
n	final nun		נוּן סוֹפִית	ן
s	samech	60	סָמֶךְ	ס
—	ayin	70	עַיִן	ע
p	pay	80	פֵּא	פּ
f	fay		פֵא	פ
f	final fay		פֵּא סוֹפִית	ף
ts, tz	tzadee	90	צָדִי	צ
ts, tz	final tzadee		צָדִי סוֹפִית	ץ
k	kof	100	קוֹף	ק
r	resh	200	רֵישׁ	ר
sh	shin	300	שִׁין	שׁ
s	sin		שִׂין	שׂ
t	tav	400	תָּו	תּ
t	tav		תָו	ת

Note: The ḥ sound is variously represented in English as ch, h, ḥ, or kh (e.g., **Ch**anukah or **Ḥ**anukkah, **ch**allah or **ḥ**allah, hala**ch**ah or hala**kh**ah).

Key to pronunciation: **a** as in r**a**n, S**a**bbath; **ä** as in f**a**ther, M**a**tzah; **ā** as in p**ay**, s**e**der; **e** as in l**e**t, t**e**mple; **ē** as in dr**ea**m, H**e**brew; **ə** as in **a**bout, h**e**lpful, proph**e**t; **i** as in p**i**n, M**i**tzvah; **ī** as in f**i**ve, rabb**i**; **o** as in p**o**t, h**o**stage; **ô** as in b**ou**ght, p**o**rtion; **ō** as in b**oa**t, M**o**ses; **o͞o** as in w**oo**d, K**i**bbutz; **o͞o** as in tr**u**e, R**u**th.

x

INTRODUCTION
GOD, THE ALEF-BET, AND TRUTH

The chapters of this book about God are arranged according to the letters of the Hebrew alphabet, the alef-bet. The alef-bet is one of the first things you learned when you began your Jewish education. Your teachers taught you the alef-bet with the hope that you would soon be able to read the Hebrew prayers that Jews have addressed to God. (You can, of course, pray to God in any language.)

Many Jews believe the Hebrew alphabet is more than just a group of letters from which words are written. According to one tradition, the first words of the Book of Genesis, "In the beginning God created ..." (בְּרֵאשִׁית בָּרָא אֱלֹהִים אֵת), teach that before God created anything else He created אֵת—the letters from alef to tav. For this reason, there are some Jews who consider the alef-bet the most basic part of the whole universe!

Many Hebrew prayers call attention to the special relationship between God and the letters of the alef-bet. These prayers are called **acrostics.** Acrostics use the letters of the alef-bet in order. You may be familiar with the Ashrei (אַשְׁרֵי) prayer, for example. The first three verses of this prayer begin with the letter alef. The following verse begins with the letter bet, the next with gimmel, and so on down to tav. Another familiar acrostic prayer is "God Is Blessed and Great" (אֵל בָּרוּךְ גְּדוֹל דֵּעָה). The first twenty-two words of the prayer begin with the letters of the alef-bet in order. The songs that we sing at the end of the Passover seder also include some well-known acrostics, such as "Adir Hu," אַדִּיר הוּא.

Why were so many authors of Hebrew prayers fond of acrostics? One explanation is that acrostics remind us that God is so great that all the letters of the alef-bet are needed to praise Him fully. We could even say that just as we need every letter to praise God, we also need all our abilities to serve God.

If you write out the letters of the alef-bet, including the five final letters (chaf, mem, nun, fay, tzadee), you will see that there are twenty-seven letters in all. The middle letter, surrounded by thirteen others on each side, is mem. The first, middle, and last letters together—alef, mem, tav—spell out the Hebrew word for truth, Emet.

Each letter of the Hebrew word אֱמֶת is represented by at least one chapter in this book. One of the chapters beginning with the letter alef is itself called "Emet." This chapter describes some of the connections Jews have made between God and truth. The chapter title beginning with the letter mem, "Mashiaḥ" (מָשִׁיחַ), which means Messiah, describes the Jewish belief that we must make the world a better place. One of the chapters beginning with tav, "Tefillah" (תְּפִלָּה), which means prayer, explains a basic way for people to communicate with God.

Several other chapters describe Jewish ideas about the nature of God and how we can become connected to God. Still others show how the Jewish belief that life has a purpose relates to Jewish ways of thinking about God and His world.

Perhaps the ideas presented here will help you think of ways to make the idea of God meaningful in your own life. If you feel challenged to search for Emet in thinking about God, the world, and your own place in it, then this book will have achieved its purpose.

"Adir biMeluchah" is sung near the close of the Passover seder. You can tell that the poem is an acrostic by looking carefully at the enlarged letters on the left-hand page of this fifteenth-century Haggadah.

EMUNAH

e • m$\overline{oo}$ • nä′

Emunah means faith, belief, or trust in God. It can also mean God's faithfulness toward the people of Israel. "Amen" (אָמֵן), which means "so be it" or "it is so," is related to the Hebrew word אֱמוּנָה.

Martin Buber believed that Emunah combines what our parents teach us with what we decide on our own.

CHAPTER ONE

Throughout history, many Jews have lived through terrible times without losing their Emunah.

In 1492, for example, the Jews were driven out of Spain. According to one account, many fled on board a certain boat. Among them was a young family—a man, his wife, and their two sons. When plague spread among the passengers, the captain ordered them ashore. The mother died while still on board, and, as the father tried to carry his sons to safety, all three of them fainted with hunger. When he revived, the father discovered that his sons had died. The man then spoke these words: "God in heaven, I want you to know that in spite of all my sufferings, my faith in You is still strong. A Jew I am, and a Jew I shall remain. No matter what people do to me, I will stay loyal to You."

Despite the most dreadful event of modern times, the Holocaust, Jews maintain their faith in God. Even in the Nazi death camps, in the face of the most extreme suffering, many Jewish inmates managed to keep their Emunah.

Does a Jew have to have Emunah to be Jewish? Many people would say that Jews are Jewish more because of how they behave than because of how or what they believe. Others say that we need Emunah in order to behave Jewishly or to improve our Jewish behavior. Still others say that Jewish behavior eventually leads to Emunah. As you read this chapter and the rest of this book, you may come to your own conclusions about what role Emunah can and should play in your own life.

In this chapter, you will learn what one of our special formulas for praying has to do with Emunah. You will also read a story about how a rabbi helped another Jew resolve a problem about Emunah.

◁
"The heavens declare the glory of God, the sky proclaims His handiwork" (Psalm 19:2).

CHAPTER SUMMARY

Lesson 1: We should base our Emunah on our own ideas as well as on what our parents teach us.

Lesson 2: Statements of faith can also serve as expressions of hope.

Emunah and the Amidah

How often do you accept something as fact just because your parents tell you it is so? As you grow older, more mature, and more independent, you may be guided by what your parents say, but you properly insist on coming to your own conclusions based on your own learning and personal experience.

Every time we say the Amidah (עֲמִידָה), we address God not only as "our God" but also as "God of our fathers." As you read more about this blessing from the Amidah and what it may have to do with Emunah, ask yourself:

What may the opening blessing of the Amidah have to do with forming our own Emunah?

"OUR GOD AND GOD OF OUR FATHERS"

The first blessing of the Amidah opens with these words: "Blessed are You, Lord our God and God of our fathers, God of Abraham, God of Isaac, and God of Jacob." The Hebrew word for fathers is אָבוֹת, so this opening blessing is called **Avot.**

When this blessing was written over 2000 years ago, what did its authors have in mind? What is the point of referring to God both as "our God" and as "God of our ancestors"? The great religious thinker Martin Buber (1878–1965) had an interesting explanation.

According to Buber, some people find their Emunah as a result of studying and thinking on their own. Other people believe in God because their parents taught them to. Neither kind of Emunah by itself is perfect.

If you believe in God only because you have thought up arguments that prove He exists, someone may challenge your arguments and cause you to lose your Emunah.

If you worship God simply because your parents taught you to, your Emunah also is not perfect. It is based on love for your parents and not on love for God.

According to Buber, Emunah is perfect only if it combines both aspects: what our parents have taught us and

WHAT'S YOUR OPINION?

How can a Jew retain Emunah even while admitting that God sometimes seems to stand by silently as good people suffer? A character in a novel by Meyer Levin had this answer: "God has given us free will ... to choose between good and evil.... God could not therefore permit Himself to interfere in man's actions, for then there would be an end to free will.... This, and only this, ... can give us back a belief in God—in a compassionate, torn, and sorrowing God who gave us free will out of love, and having forbidden Himself to interfere, must behold in agony what we do with our freedom."

what we have decided on our own. When we say "our God," we show that our own studying and thinking have led us to believe in Him. When we say "God of our fathers," we show that we believe in Him also because of tradition.

Buber also explained why we say "God of Abraham, God of Isaac, and God of Jacob" and not simply "God of Abraham, Isaac, and Jacob." The wording of the blessing shows that Isaac came to his own belief in God. Isaac did not accept God merely because his father Abraham did (although his father's belief in God set an important example for him). In the same way, Jacob also found his own belief in God. His personal belief strengthened the belief he inherited from his parents and grandparents.

THINK ABOUT IT

1. What is one explanation for the fact that the Avot blessing refers both to "our God" and to "God of our fathers"?

2. Some prayerbooks and many congregations today have changed the text of Avot to include our female ancestors as well: "God of Abraham and of Sarah, God of Isaac and of Rebecca, God of Jacob and of Leah and Rachel." What does this change show about Jewish beliefs and prayers?

3. Name one belief of your parents that you accept without challenging, and one belief of theirs that you disagree with.

4. Explain in your own words the meaning behind the idea that God shows His Emunah by giving us the freedom to choose good or evil.

Jews kept their Emunah even when expelled from Spain in 1492.

A prayer for Emunah

Jews have never been required to accept any statement of Emunah. The Thirteen Principles of Emunah of the great Jewish thinker Moses Maimonides (1135–1204) do appear in the prayerbook, however. These principles include the beliefs that God is one, that the whole Torah was given by God to Moses, that Moses was the greatest of the prophets, and that the Mashiaḥ will come.

As you read a story about Maimonides' Thirteen Principles, ask yourself the following question:

How is the meaning of Maimonides' words "I believe with perfect faith" changed if we consider them as a prayer instead of a statement of fact?

PRAYING FOR COMPLETE EMUNAH

Rabbi Noah of Lechovitz lived in an apartment that shared a wall with the House of Study. One day, while the rabbi was in his room, he overheard the voice of a man next door who was saying Maimonides' Thirteen Principles of Emunah. Each time he recited the words "I believe with perfect faith"—the words that introduce each principle—the man would stop and whisper to himself, "I don't understand that! I don't understand that!"

Rabbi Noah was curious to find out what the man didn't understand, so he went next door to ask him.

"The words 'I believe with perfect faith' are giving me trouble, rabbi," the man said. "If I truly believe with perfect faith, then how can I explain the fact that I sin, as I know I do? But if I sin because I don't truly believe the words I'm saying, then why am I making matters worse by lying, and saying that I *do* believe with perfect faith?"

Rabbi Noah offered these words of advice. "Think of Maimonides' words not as a statement but as a prayer. Each time you say 'I believe with perfect faith,' what you are really saying is, 'I hope that I may come to believe!'"

THINK ABOUT IT

1. Which five English words begin each of the Thirteen Principles?

2. According to Rabbi Noah, what do the words really mean?

3. Why is it possible for us to pray even if we have trouble believing in God with a "perfect faith"?

4. Do you think there are *any* beliefs that a Jew must hold in order to be a Jew? If so, what are they?

אֱמֶת

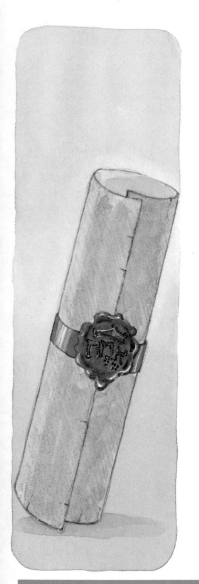

EMET

e • met′

Emet means truth. People must show Emet in dealing with one another. Emet is also part of the nature of God.

Emet is God's personal seal, said the rabbis of the Talmud.

CHAPTER TWO

Centuries ago, a group of children came to a study hall where some of the greatest rabbis were studying. The children amazed the rabbis by their inventive explanations of what each letter of the alef-bet stood for. When they reached the last two letters, they said that שׁ stood for Sheker (שֶׁקֶר), or falsehood, while ת stood for Emet (אֱמֶת), or truth.

The children explained that שֶׁקֶר has three of the last four letters of the alef-bet because so often one lie leads right to another. Because people speak Emet only from time to time, Emet is much less common than Sheker. For that reason, the letters of אֱמֶת are spread out through the entire alef-bet.

The children then asked the rabbis to notice that in Torah script, each letter of שׁקר rests insecurely on only one foot, while all three letters of אמת have a solid foundation. This difference, explained the children, shows that falsehood will eventually be toppled, but truth can support the world on its firm footing.

You, too, know how important a solid foundation of truth really is. After someone has lied to you, isn't it hard to rely on anything that person says?

In this chapter, you will learn how the rabbis of the Talmud connected God with Emet. You will also read a story about practicing Emet in dealing with other people.

CHAPTER SUMMARY

Lesson 1: Emet is one aspect of the nature of God.

Lesson 2: Honesty in dealings with other people is an important kind of Emet.

Emet is an aspect of God

◁
Sheker, or falsehood, totters on a shaky base, while Emet stands on a firm foundation.

Nowadays, when you finish writing a letter, you address an envelope, add your return address, and seal the envelope by wetting the glue on its flap. But in times past, you would have closed the letter with a wafer of melted wax. You would have then pressed your own personal stone or metal seal into the wax. The person receiving the letter would see your seal and know that the letter came from you. The rabbis of the Talmud used the image of a personal seal as one way of showing how closely God is related to Emet. They said that Emet is God's personal seal. As you read more about the ways Jews have associated God with Emet, ask yourself these questions:

(a) How is the relationship between God and Emet made clear in the traditional service?
(b) How does the Hebrew word אֱמֶת *suggest that God is King forever?*

"THE LORD YOUR GOD IS TRUE"

In the traditional service, the connection between God and Emet is made clear every day. The final words of the full Shema are "I am the Lord your God." The first word of the prayer that follows is "Emet," or "true." We do not usually pause between the end of the Shema and the beginning of the following prayer. By running the two prayers together, the worshipers say "the Lord your God is true," יְיָ אֱלֹהֵיכֶם אֱמֶת.

EMET AS AN ACRONYM

Both in English and in Hebrew, it is not unusual for new words to be formed from the first letters of several other words. The word "radar" was formed by putting together the words "**ra**dio **d**etecting **a**nd **r**anging." The word "laser" was made from "**l**ight **a**mplification by **s**timulated **e**mission of **r**adiation." Words like "radar" and "laser" are called **acronyms.**

In the same way, the rabbis thought that the word אֱמֶת might be an acronym. The א stands for one of the Hebrew words for God: אֱלֹהִים. The מ stands for the Hebrew word for King: מֶלֶךְ. The ת stands for the Hebrew word meaning Eternal: תָּמִיד. These three Hebrew words together mean "God is King forever."

By interpreting the word אֱמֶת as an acronym, the rabbis

HAVE YOU HEARD?

You use the word מֶלֶךְ every time you make a blessing. You may also recognize the word תָּמִיד from the נֵר תָּמִיד, or eternal light, which always burns in the synagogue.

showed how the firm foundation of truth is related to the firm foundation of God's lasting rule.

THINK ABOUT IT

1. How does the way the Shema is said in traditional services stress the connection between God and Emet?

2. According to the rabbis, the word אֱמֶת is an acronym of which three Hebrew words?

3. Describe a time when a friend lied to you. How did you feel when you found out?

Emet in action

Judaism teaches that one way people can draw close to God is by behaving in a Godlike way. Since Emet is one of God's aspects, people can imitate God by being honest in all their dealings. As you read a story about a fourth-century Babylonian rabbi who practiced Emet, ask yourself:

How did Rabbi Safra show that human beings practice Emet by being faithful to God and honest with people?

TRUTH AND THE SALE OF A DONKEY

One morning, Rabbi Safra was outside, saying his prayers as usual. He was in the middle of the Shema when a man came up to him.

"I understand you want to sell your donkey, rabbi," said the man. "If that fine-looking beast over there is the animal in question, I'll give you fifty shekels for him."

Rabbi Safra did want to sell his donkey, and fifty shekels was exactly the price he was hoping for. But he didn't want to stop while reciting the Shema, so he gave no answer.

The man misunderstood the rabbi's silence, however. He thought it meant that the price he had offered was too low. So the man raised his offer. "I'll give you sixty shekels," he said.

Just as the word "laser" is an English acronym for "light amplification by stimulated emission of radiation," so the rabbis thought of אֱמֶת as a Hebrew acronym for אֱלֹהִים מֶלֶךְ תָּמִיד, "God is King forever."

We imitate God when we are honest and truthful with others.

Still Rabbi Safra said nothing. So the man raised his offer again. "I'll give you seventy shekels for the donkey, but not a shekel more."

By now Rabbi Safra had finished the Shema. Even though the offer of seventy shekels was tempting, the rabbi refused to take more than the original price.

"My friend," said the rabbi, "I had every intention of selling you the donkey for your first offer. But I didn't want to answer you before I completed the Shema and added the word 'Emet' that follows in the next prayer. It would have been disrespectful to God to interrupt my prayers. But it would make a mockery of the words 'The Lord your God is true' if I now took advantage of the situation to accept more money from you."

THINK ABOUT IT

1. Explain Rabbi Safra's silence when the man first offered him fifty shekels for the donkey.

2. How does this story show that telling the truth means more than just not lying?

בּוֹרֵא אֶת הַכֹּל

BORAY ET HAKOL

bô•rā′ et hä•kōl′

Boray et HaKol means "Creator of all things." Included in Boray et HaKol are the beliefs that God created the world and that everything was created for a purpose.

David learned that even "useless" creatures like the wasp and the spider were created for a purpose.

15

Many stories in the Midrash teach that God is Boray et HaKol. One story tells about the Roman Emperor Hadrian's claims to godhood.

Hadrian returned to Rome after one of his victories. He said to his courtiers, "Since I have successfully conquered the world, I want you to treat me as God."

The Emperor's arrogance did not sit well with his courtiers. But how could they oppose him without risking their lives? After a while, the court philosopher thought of a plan.

"Your Highness," said the philosopher, "I have a problem I beg you to help me solve. A ship carrying all my worldly goods is three miles out at sea, threatened by a storm."

Hadrian answered, "I will gladly send out several Roman legions to rescue your ship."

"But they might not get there in time," the philosopher said. "Why don't you send a puff of wind to change the course of the storm?"

"Nonsense!" said the Emperor. "Where can I get wind to send?"

"Well, then," the philosopher replied, "why should we treat you as God, Who created the wind along with everything else?"

In this chapter, you will read two more stories that picture God as Boray et HaKol. The first tells how Rabbi Akiba (c. 50–135 C.E.) taught a nonbeliever that God is Boray et HaKol. The second story teaches that everything that God created serves a purpose.

◁
One look at this delicate sixteenth-century tapestry should convince you it didn't just happen by chance. Similarly, some people think the world around us is so intricate and so beautiful that it, too, must have a Maker.

CHAPTER SUMMARY

Lesson 1: The world can be seen as evidence of a Creator.

Lesson 2: Everything God created serves a purpose.

Every product has a producer

Some people wonder about the story of Creation as told in the Book of Genesis. After all, science teaches us that the world has been evolving over billions of years. So how can the story that the world was created in six days also be true?

"He sends forth His word to the earth; His command runs swiftly. He lays down snow like fleece, scatters frost like ashes" (Psalm 147:15–16).

In fact, the rabbis themselves believed that the literal meaning of the Creation story was only a first step in understanding God as Boray et HaKol. Rashi (1040–1105), the greatest of all Bible interpreters, goes to great lengths to show that the first chapter of Genesis does not lay out the events of Creation in a specific order. Still, the rabbis had no doubt that the Bible accurately portrayed God as the Creator of all things. As you read the following story about Rabbi Akiba and a nonbeliever, look for an answer to this question:

How did Akiba show that God is Boray et HaKol?

RABBI AKIBA'S PROOF

A Roman came to Akiba one day and challenged the rabbi to come up with clear proof that God had created the world. Akiba told him to return the next day.

When the Roman returned, Akiba said to him, "What are you wearing?" Surprised by the question, the Roman answered, "A suit of clothes."

"Do you know who made the fabric for your suit?" asked the rabbi.

"A weaver did," the Roman answered.

"I don't believe you," said Rabbi Akiba. "You'll have to come up with clear proof that a weaver made the fabric for your clothes."

The Roman didn't know what to make of this challenge.

"What kind of proof can I give you? The fabric didn't just get here by itself. Isn't it obvious that a weaver wove the fabric?"

Akiba then said, "Isn't it just as obvious that God created the world?"

As the Roman sheepishly turned and left, Akiba's students asked him to explain himself further.

"My students," said Akiba, "just as there can be no house without a builder and no fabric without a weaver, so there could be no world without God, Boray et HaKol."

THINK ABOUT IT

1. How did Rabbi Akiba try to convince the Roman that the world had to have a Creator?

2. Do you think that Rabbi Akiba's argument is convincing proof or not? Explain your answer.

3. Name one fact you accept as true without being able to prove it.

All Creation serves a purpose

Many of us have gazed up at the heavens on a beautiful starry night and been filled with awe at the majesty of Creation. But have you ever been awakened by the sound of a mosquito buzzing in your ear, and wondered what earthly purpose such a pest could possibly serve? The rabbis understood that most people had thoughts like this from time to time, but the rabbis also insisted that God carries out His purpose through everything, even fleas, gnats, and frogs. Read a story about how King David (c. 1000 B.C.E.) learned this lesson as a young man, and ask:

How did David learn that God creates everything for a purpose?

DAVID, THE WASP, AND THE SPIDER

As David sat in his garden one day, he saw a wasp eating a spider. "God," he said, "why have You created these useless creatures? The wasp gives no honey and looks ugly. The spi-

WHAT'S YOUR OPINION?

The eleventh-century philosopher Baḥya ibn Pakuda used another striking image in seeking to prove the existence of a Creator. He said: "If, by accident, ink spilled out onto a blank sheet of paper, the result would never be legible writing. Whoever showed us a page of beautifully written script and said it resulted from an ink spill would be called a liar. How, then, can anyone claim that the world, which is so much more intricate in its design than a page of script, came about without the purpose, power, and wisdom of a wise and powerful Designer?"

der just wastes its time. All day long it weaves and weaves, but its web never becomes useful fabric."

Then God answered David, "The time will come when you will learn that I have created nothing without good reason."

Shortly thereafter, David learned that King Saul was plotting to kill him. David was forced to flee. He found a good hiding place—a dark cave in the wilderness. Once David was safely inside, God had a spider spin a web to cover the entrance to the cave.

When Saul and his soldiers approached the cave in search of David, they saw the web over the cave's mouth. "At least we know he's not hiding in there," said one of them. "No one could get through that web without tearing it."

Later, David decided to send some of his men to learn where Saul and his soldiers had set up camp. Having found out Saul's location, David went there by night. He discovered King Saul and his followers fast asleep around the fire. The king's head rested on a leather bag containing water. Saul's spear was stuck in the earth near his head. Nearby slept Saul's general, Abner, with his long legs curled up under him.

David did not want to harm King Saul, but he did want to leave some sign that he had been there. So he crept up and carefully removed the king's spear and the waterskin on which Saul's head lay. Suddenly, Abner stretched his long legs as he slept. David was now trapped.

Overcome by fear, David silently prayed to God. No sooner had he finished his prayer than a wasp settled on Abner's leg and stung the general. Still sleeping, Abner jerked his legs back, and David was able to make his escape.

David had now learned that all God's creatures serve a purpose. Even the spider and the wasp can help carry out the will of God, Boray et HaKol.

THINK ABOUT IT

1. David already knew that God was Boray et HaKol, but what lesson did he still have to learn?

2. How can you extend the moral of this story so it applies to our feelings toward other human beings?

HAVE YOU HEARD?

Writers of Jewish history use B.C.E. (Before the Common Era) to mean what Christian writers mean by B.C. (Before Christ). Similarly, Jews use the abbreviation C.E. (Common Era) instead of the Christian A.D. (a Latin phrase meaning "In the year of our Lord"). The abbreviation c. stands for *circa*, a Latin word that means "about" or "around."

SEE FOR YOURSELF

You can find the Biblical story on which the legend of David, the wasp, and the spider is based at I Samuel 24, 26. For an example of how frogs and insects can serve God's purposes, read the description of the plagues brought against Egypt, especially Exodus 7:25–8:20.

בַּל תַּשְׁחִית

BAL TASHḤIT
bäl′ täsh • ḥēt′

Bal Tashḥit means "do not destroy." This idea underlies the Jewish concern for the environment. It also encourages us to care for other living things. People become partners in the act of Creation when they observe Bal Tashḥit.

You can practice Bal Tashḥit by keeping our parks clean.

CHAPTER FOUR

Young people can sometimes open up the eyes of adults. As Rabbi Joshua ben Ḥananiah went out walking one day, he found what seemed to be a path across a field. Innocently, he began to cut across the path. All of a sudden, he heard a girl calling after him.

"Rabbi, can't you see that you're trampling our crops? This farm is ours, and, you have no right to cut across it."

"Young lady," he answered, "I clearly see a path that other feet have created."

"The feet that have trampled this so-called path," said the young girl, "belong to people who think only of their own convenience and care nothing for Bal Tashḥit."

In this chapter, you will learn some ideas related to Bal Tashḥit. The first section explores the idea that human beings are only caretakers of God's world. In the second section you will learn two different ways of observing Bal Tashḥit.

CHAPTER SUMMARY

Lesson 1: Human beings don't own the world. They are only caretakers of God's world.

Lesson 2: Bal Tashḥit can be observed by not doing destructive acts and by performing constructive ones.

The earth belongs to God

Imagine that you own an apartment building. You hire a caretaker to make sure the building stays in good shape. How would you feel if your caretaker broke the windows, wrote graffiti on the walls, and left trash in the hallways? We expect caretakers, gardeners, and housekeepers to care for the things of this world. Now think about our responsibility to protect the earth. Look for an answer to this question as you read on:

How do the stories about Adam in the Torah and the Midrash show concern for the environment?

WHAT'S YOUR OPINION?

The story about Rabbi Joshua ben Ḥananiah also teaches another lesson: don't blindly follow what others do. Always consider beforehand what your actions might lead to. Can you think of ways this lesson might relate to environmental issues like toxic waste dumping, nuclear weapons testing, and the hunting of whales and other rare species?

◁

What Rabbi Joshua ben Ḥananiah thought was a public walkway was actually just a path that other feet had trampled.

CARETAKERS OF GOD'S WORLD

According to the Torah, after God created Adam and Eve, He told them to rule over all the earth and its contents. When we read the Torah closely, we can see that God wasn't giving human beings the right to do anything they want to the environment. God put Adam in the garden of Eden "to work it and to guard it." From these words we learn that the garden remained God's property. Adam's job was to treat it with care and protect it from damage.

A Midrash about Adam shows how concerned the rabbis were about Bal Tashḥit. The Midrash says that after God created Adam, He walked him through the Garden of Eden, showing him all the trees.

"Look how beautiful all of Creation is," said God. "But take care not to destroy My world, for if you do, no one after you will be able to set it right."

According to another old Midrash, when God was about to create Adam, many angels tried to talk Him out of it. A modern version of this Midrash says that among the outspoken opponents of God's plan were several angels in charge

Recycling paper helps reduce waste and preserve the earth's resources. This Swiss team collected forty tons of paper in a single day.

of the earth's resources. These angels all argued that humankind would violate Bal Tashhit by polluting the air and water and by damaging all growing things.

Despite all these protests, God created people because He knew they could help make a better world.

THINK ABOUT IT

1. Some people blame the Creation story for giving people the idea they can take anything they want from nature. What statement in the Torah leads them to say that? How would you refute their argument?

2. Compare the message of groups who warn about the dangers of nuclear weapons with the warning God made to Adam in the Midrash.

Two ways of observing Bal Tashhit

Imagine that your parents are leaving you in charge of your younger brothers or sisters for a while. Their parting words to you are "Take care of them." There are two ways you can carry out their wishes. One is to avoid doing anything to bother the children, such as teasing. Another way is to organize a constructive activity you can all do together, such as baking a cake. In a similar way, Bal Tashhit can be observed negatively, by *not doing* something that will *harm* the environment, or positively, by *doing* something that will *improve* the environment. As you read the next two stories, ask yourself:

How do the stories about Rabbi Elazar and Honi teach negative and positive ways of observing Bal Tashhit?

DON'T HARM THE ENVIRONMENT—DO IMPROVE IT

One day Rabbi Elazar and Rabbi Shimon ben Kahana were taking a walk after lunch. As they talked, Rabbi Elazar saw a beautiful patch of wild flowers near the roadside. Rabbi Elazar suddenly had the idea of picking a bunch of flowers to

SEE FOR YOURSELF

Both the Torah and the Talmud contain antipollution laws and other laws dealing with Bal Tashhit. Deuteronomy 20:19–20 and 23:13–15 teach that even in wartime, soldiers must not destroy fruit trees and must dispose of sewage properly. Laws in the Talmud deal with soil conservation, garbage disposal, and air pollution.

bring back home, and he asked Rabbi Shimon to help him gather a bouquet.

Before Rabbi Shimon could start picking, however, Rabbi Elazar thought better of the idea. "Think about it," he said. "If everybody went and picked wild flowers, eventually there would be no flowers left for anyone to enjoy."

Another story teaches a lesson about a more positive kind of Bal Tashḥit, which involves taking active steps to improve the environment. One day Ḥoni set out from home with a picnic lunch. As he was walking along the side of the road, he saw a man planting a carob tree. Ḥoni asked the man, "How long will it take before the tree you are planting will bear fruit?"

The man answered, "Seventy years."

Ḥoni then asked, "Do you expect to be around to eat this tree's fruit seventy years from now?"

The man told him, "I will be dead by then. But just as my ancestors planted trees whose fruit I enjoy today, so I am planting trees for the generations who will live after me."

By now, Ḥoni was hungry, so he had his picnic. Then he decided to take a nap. What Ḥoni didn't know was that this nap would last for a full seventy years!

When Ḥoni awoke from his sleep, he saw a man gathering fruit from the very carob tree he had just seen planted. Confused, Ḥoni asked, "Excuse me, sir, are you the man who planted this tree?"

"No," the man answered. "My grandfather planted this tree seventy years ago. Every generation of our family tries to improve the environment in some way for the benefit of those who come after us. I found ready-grown carob trees in the world. As my contribution to Bal Tashḥit, I am planting new carob trees for my children and grandchildren."

Rabbi Elazar realized that if everyone picked wild flowers, there would be no flowers left for anyone to enjoy.

THINK ABOUT IT

1. Name one difference and one similarity between the kinds of Bal Tashḥit described in the stories about Rabbi Elazar and Ḥoni.

2. Describe one negative and one positive way you can observe Bal Tashḥit.

בַּר מִצְוָה, בַּת מִצְוָה

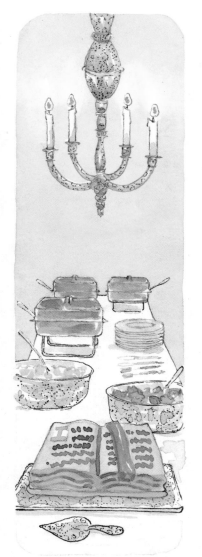

BAR MITZVAH, BAT MITZVAH

bär′ mits • vä′, bät′ mits • vä′

Bar Mitzvah and **Bat Mitzvah** can be translated as "man of obligation" and "woman of obligation." A person who is Bar or Bat Mitzvah is old enough to be responsible for performing the Mitzvot. According to tradition, boys reach that age at thirteen, and girls at twelve or thirteen.

You celebrate your Bar or Bat Mitzvah for a day, but the responsibilities you take on last a lifetime.

One sign that becoming Bar or Bat Mitzvah signals the onset of new adult responsibilities is the blessing that parents may recite at the service: "Blessed is He Who frees me from responsibility for this child."

בָּרוּךְ שֶׁפְּטָרַנִי מֵעָנְשׁוֹ שֶׁל זֶה.

The prayer means that the child is now directly accountable to other people and to God for his or her own behavior.

◁

In receiving the Torah from her father, this Bat Mitzvah accepts her adult Jewish religious responsibilities.

When you think about becoming Bar or Bat Mitzvah, what thoughts come to mind? As you turn thirteen, many changes are going on in your life. Some are physical changes, which indicate that your body is becoming more mature. Some are emotional and intellectual changes, which also show that you are no longer a child. You and your friends may have new interests. You may notice that your teachers and parents expect more of you and that you have new responsibilities at home and at school. You may feel differently about the adults in your life.

It is clear that someone who has reached the age of twelve or thirteen has entered a new stage in life. Many cultures have special ceremonies to mark this new stage. In Judaism, the ceremony is the Bar or Bat Mitzvah. It is designed for young people who, though they are still children in many ways, are ready to take on new religious responsibilities.

In this chapter you will learn that Bat Mitzvah celebrations are a recent tradition, and that Bar Mitzvah celebrations, too, began later than you might think. You will also read about some newsworthy Bar and Bat Mitzvah celebrations.

CHAPTER SUMMARY

Lesson 1: The tradition of Bar and Bat Mitzvah celebrations is quite new, but the ages of twelve and thirteen have been important in Judaism since the time of the Talmud and Midrash.

Lesson 2: Bar and Bat Mitzvah celebrations can take unusual forms and have very special meanings.

A lifetime role, not just a one-day party

When you graduate from elementary school to junior high or from junior high to high school, the ceremony is often called "commencement," which is another way of saying "beginning." Each commencement ceremony marks your passage into a new role in life. The day you celebrate your Bar or Bat

Mitzvah is likewise a commencement. On that day you take on a new role as a Jew. As you read more about the difference between Bar or Bat Mitzvah as a lifetime role and as a ceremony, ask yourself:

(a) What is the difference between Bar and Bat Mitzvah as a celebration and as a time of changing obligations?
(b) According to the Midrash, how did Abraham and Jacob mark their commitment to God at age thirteen?

YOU REMAIN BAR OR BAT MITZVAH FOR LIFE

No one in the Bible or Talmud had the kind of Bar or Bat Mitzvah celebration that is so familiar to us. But the idea that at thirteen a Jew enters a new stage in life dates back to the days of the Talmud. Judah ben Tema, who lived about 1800 years ago, said: "At thirteen the age is reached for the fulfillment of the Mitzvot." Once you turn thirteen, for example, you can be counted as one of the ten adults needed to form a Minyan.

HAVE YOU HEARD?

The custom of celebrating a Bar Mitzvah with a festive service followed by a party and gifts is only a few centuries old. The Bat Mitzvah celebration is even more recent. The first Bat Mitzvah ceremony in the United States, that of Judith Kaplan (see page 33), took place in 1922.

A young man prepares for his Bar Mitzvah service by choosing the Tallit he will wear on the big day.

The Talmud also teaches that once a girl has turned twelve or a boy has turned thirteen, she or he is required to fast on Yom Kippur. This Mitzvah remains a Jew's responsibility from that age on. In another passage, the Talmud uses the term "Bar Mitzvah" to mean every adult Jew, not just a boy of thirteen.

AGE THIRTEEN AS A TURNING POINT IN THE MIDRASH

You probably know the story about Abraham in his father's idol shop. While Abraham was minding the store one day, he decided he could no longer pretend to accept his father's beliefs. He decided instead to make a clear statement of his belief in the One God. So he smashed the idols. When his father returned and asked what had happened, Abraham told him the idols had argued among themselves.

Nonsense, said his father, idols were only clay figures and incapable of argument. "Then why pray to them?" asked Abraham. According to the Midrash, Abraham was thirteen at the time of this event.

Another Midrash marks thirteen as a turning point in the lives of Jacob and Esau. From the time his twin sons were little, Isaac had made sure that both received the same good education. But when the boys turned thirteen, Esau went to worship idols. Jacob, on the other hand, marked his commitment to God by going to the House of Study.

THINK ABOUT IT

1. The idea that a person becomes Bar Mitzvah at age thirteen and remains Bar Mitzvah for the rest of his life was first suggested in (a) 1922 (b) the Torah (c) the Talmud.

2. How did Abraham and Jacob show that the age of thirteen can mark a turning point in a Jew's commitment to God?

3. What are two things you can do after your Bar or Bat Mitzvah to show that you have entered a new stage of Jewish life?

Three unusual celebrations

In most Jewish families, a child's Bar or Bat Mitzvah celebration is a great event. But some celebrations are so extraordinary that they take on special meaning even for people outside the family. As you read about three such Bar and Bat Mitzvah celebrations, ask yourself:

What made each of these three Bar and Bat Mitzvah celebrations special in its own way?

This richly decorated Torah case lends beauty to a Bar Mitzvah celebration in Israel. Each side of the hinged cover shows the Ten Commandments, or Aseret HaDibrot.

HAVE YOU HEARD?

Some adults, for one reason or another, were not able to have a Bar or Bat Mitzvah celebration when they were younger. (They became obligated to perform the Mitzvot anyway.) Today many such adults celebrate a belated Bar or Bat Mitzvah as a way of marking a new or renewed commitment to Judaism.

An adult Bat Mitzvah in California.

THE FIRST BAT MITZVAH IN THE UNITED STATES

Judith Kaplan came from no ordinary home. Her father was Mordecai Kaplan (1881–1983), an influential professor at the Jewish Theological Seminary in New York City. He was to become the founder of the Reconstructionist movement of Judaism. Kaplan's efforts led to many aspects of Jewish life that we take for granted today. For example, Kaplan thought up the idea of the modern Jewish synagogue center, where not only prayer and study but also athletics, children's activities, and community events could take place in a Jewish setting.

In the spring between Judith's twelfth and thirteenth birthdays, her father decided it was time to put into practice one of his beliefs: that women could and should have an equal role in Jewish religious life. Judith's Bat Mitzvah took place in New York, at Rabbi Kaplan's newly founded Society for the Advancement of Judaism.

Judith later became a well-known musicologist. As an adult, she recalled that after reading her selection from the weekly portion along with the blessings before and after the Torah reading, "no thunder sounded, no lightning struck."

It has taken many years for the Bat Mitzvah ceremony to achieve full equality with the Bar Mitzvah. But Judith Kaplan's Bat Mitzvah was the first step.

AN AMERICAN BAR MITZVAH IN POLAND

Before the Holocaust, the Polish city of Cracow had a Jewish community of 60,000. In 1985, only 600 Jews—none of them young—lived there. A leader of Cracow's Jewish community asked that some American Jewish families hold their sons' Bar Mitzvah celebrations in Cracow. In that way, the Jews of Cracow could once again see a young Jew participate in Jewish life.

That's how Eric Strom from Stamford, Connecticut, became the first young man in more than twenty years to celebrate his Bar Mitzvah in Cracow. The ceremony took place there in September 1985.

Eric's Haftarah from the Book of Isaiah tells of a future time when there will be no more violence. Eric understood that his portion was especially meaningful because of the history of the place where he recited it. Not far from Cracow, the Nazis had murdered hundreds of thousands of Jews at the Auschwitz death camp. Eric's own great-great-grandparents were among those victims.

By agreeing to celebrate his Bar Mitzvah in unfamiliar Cracow instead of in familiar Connecticut, Eric showed a special kind of commitment to the renewal of Jewish life.

A COMPUTERIZED BAR MITZVAH

In November 1985, Lee Kweller of Pittsburgh, Pennsylvania, celebrated a truly remarkable Bar Mitzvah. Lee, who suffers from cerebral palsy, usually communicates only through sign language. For the occasion of his Bar Mitzvah, a computer scientist designed special programs for two computers. The programs made it possible for Lee to type his portion and the appropriate blessings on a keyboard, so that a computer could make the correct Hebrew sounds. In the same way, he recited a psalm and a hymn and delivered his Bar Mitzvah address in English. In that address, Lee said, "I have come to life today, both in the tradition of my forefathers and in a very special way. I am now able to speak with all of you. This marks the beginning of a new world for me."

Most Bar and Bat Mitzvah celebrations aren't as unusual or newsworthy as Judith Kaplan's, Eric Strom's, and Lee Kweller's. But as you study and plan for your big day, try to think of ways in which the event can mark a turning point in your own life.

THINK ABOUT IT

1. In what way did Judith Kaplan's Bat Mitzvah and Eric Strom's and Lee Kweller's Bar Mitzvah celebrations mark "the beginning of a new world" either for them personally or for Jews in general?

2. What kind of personal commitment to Judaism would you like your Bar or Bat Mitzvah to represent?

HAVE YOU HEARD?

On the occasion of their Bar or Bat Mitzvah, many young people show their support for less fortunate Jews and their commitment to religious freedom by having the name of a young Soviet Jew called along with their own at the time of the Torah reading. The American Bar or Bat Mitzvah thus becomes a proxy or twin for the Soviet Jew, who is not permitted to celebrate an official Bar or Bat Mitzvah in the Soviet Union. Some Bar or Bat Mitzvah families give a percentage of the cost of the celebration to charities that feed or house the poor.

BRIT

bə• rēt

A **Brit** is a covenant or agreement. Jewish tradition describes three occasions when God entered into a Brit with humanity.

Brit means "agreement."

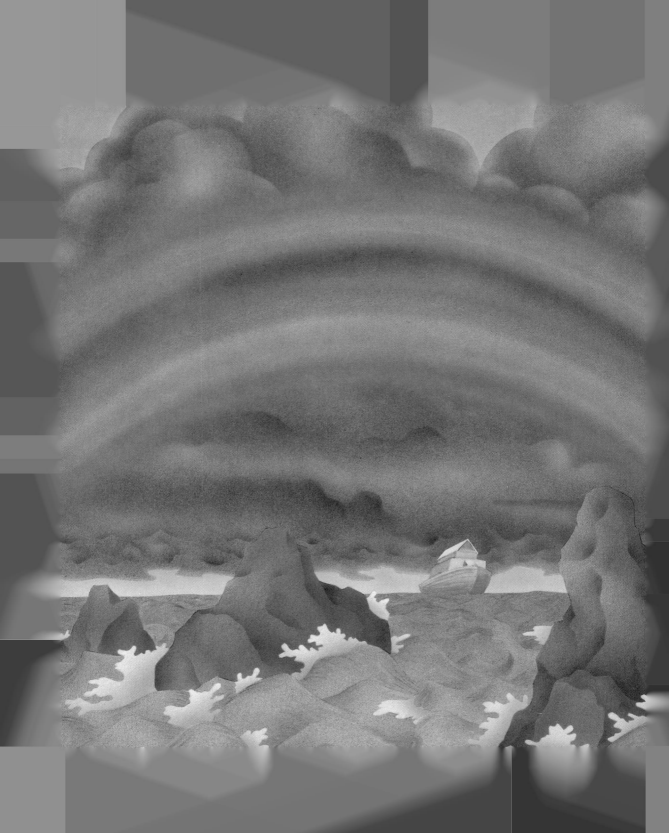

CHAPTER SIX

Do you remember your earliest friendship? Perhaps you and your friend agreed to exchange toys or to take turns playing your favorite games. The two of you may even have had a particular greeting or a secret handshake that made your relationship special. If so, your first friendship was based on a Brit. Later you may have joined a club or other group based on a Brit that set out exactly what each member must do.

Adult life is filled with examples of Brit. A contract to rent an apartment or buy a house is a Brit. When a man and a woman marry, they too make a type of Brit. Even heads of countries may make a Brit. An example of this kind of Brit is the peace agreement signed in 1979 by Egyptian President Anwar Sadat and Israeli Prime Minister Menaḥem Begin.

Often a Brit is between equals, but it does not have to be. For example, parents may offer their children a raise in allowance if the children will agree to do additional chores. Your teacher may enter into a Brit with your class: if all the class members hand in all their homework faithfully during the week, no homework will be assigned over the weekend. Or the class may suggest that the teacher agree not to give quizzes on Mondays.

In this chapter, you will learn about three times God entered into a Brit with humanity. You will also learn that each Brit has a sign that reminds each party of its obligations.

CHAPTER SUMMARY

Lesson 1: The rainbow and Shabbat are two signs of Brit between God and people.

Lesson 2: Circumcision is a sign of the Brit between God and the Jewish people.

◁

"The rainbow shall be in the clouds. When I see it, it will remind Me of the eternal Brit between God and all living things on earth" (Genesis 9:16).

ר

Two signs of Brit

Many companies have a familiar logo—a symbol that identifies them. For example, a major computer company uses a multicolored apple, and one of the television networks uses a peacock. These logos remind us of the company's responsibility to provide the public with quality service. In a similar way, the signs of Brit are intended to remind whoever sees them of the relationship between God and human beings. As you read about two signs of Brit, look for answers to these questions:

*(a) **What role does the rainbow play as a sign of Brit?***
*(b) **How does Shabbat serve as a sign of Brit?***

THE RAINBOW AS A SIGN OF BRIT

According to the Torah, after the great flood that wiped out the world's evils, God showed Noah the rainbow as a sign of Brit. The parties to this Brit were God, on the one hand, and the earth and all its present and future inhabitants, on the other.

God's description of the meaning of the rainbow shows that it serves mainly to remind Him of His responsibility to the world:

And it shall come to pass, when I cover the earth with clouds, the rainbow shall be seen in them. Then will I remember the Brit that I have made between Myself and you and all kinds of living things. Never again shall the waters become a flood to destroy all living things. The rainbow shall be in the clouds. When I see it, it will remind Me of the eternal Brit between God and all living things on earth (Genesis 9:13—16).

SHABBAT AS A SIGN OF BRIT

During Moses' forty-day stay on top of Mount Sinai, says the Torah, God told him that Shabbat would serve as a sign of Brit. The parties to this Brit were God and the Israelites.

God's description of Shabbat as a sign of Brit shows that it serves mainly to remind the Israelites of their obligation to God:

The Lord spoke to Moses and said, "Tell the Israelites: Above all you shall observe Shabbat, for Shabbat is a sign between Me and you in every generation that you may know that I am

A common kind of Brit binds families and friends to share the chores as well as the fruits of their labor.

the Lord Who makes you holy.... The Israelites shall keep Shabbat, to observe Shabbat as an eternal Brit. It is a sign between Me and the Children of Israel for ever, for in six days the Lord made heaven and earth, and on the seventh day He stopped work and was refreshed (Exodus 31:12−13, 16−17).

You may know a song to the original Hebrew words of this passage, which is called **Veshamru** (וְשָׁמְרוּ). We read the passage during the Amidah on Shabbat morning and again as part of the Kiddush at the end of Shabbat morning service.

THINK ABOUT IT

1. In the Brit that has the rainbow for a sign, which party has the greater obligation?

2. In the Brit that has Shabbat for a sign, which party has the greater obligation?

3. Discuss some agreements you have made that you might call Brit.

BRIT MILAH

Soon after a Jewish child is born, special ceremonies show that the baby belongs to the Jewish people. For a girl, the ceremony—which is called Brit Bat (בְּרִית בַּת)—may include naming the baby and giving her a ritual bath. For a boy, the ceremony of welcoming is called Brit Milah (בְּרִית מִילָה).

"Milah" is the Hebrew word for **circumcision** (sûr • kəm • sizh′ən), a ritual performed on Jewish boys when they are eight days old. During this operation, a fold of skin that extends over the tip of the penis is removed by a **Mohel** (mō • hāl′), or ritual circumciser. Although the correct name for the ritual is Brit Milah, it is often called Brit (or Bris) for short.

Below: the Brit Milah ceremony in eighteenth-century France. Right: a two-seated circumcision bench made in Germany in 1803.

According to the Torah, Brit Milah is the sign of an agreement between God and the Jewish people. God's obligation through this Brit was to keep Abraham's offspring fruitful forever and to give them the land of Canaan. The obligation of Abraham's offspring was to show their continuing loyalty to God by circumcising their sons. Think about these questions as you read more about Brit Milah:

(a) Why is circumcision an appropriate sign for this Brit?
(b) Why is Elijah the Prophet associated with Brit Milah?

CIRCUMCISION AS A SIGN OF BRIT

Why did God choose circumcision as a sign of His Brit with Abraham's descendants? Some scholars answer that by following the Mitzvah to circumcise the body part that helps create future generations, Jews show that those generations will continue in their loyalty to God.

According to one Midrash, a Roman official once made fun of the idea of circumcision. "If your God wanted you to be circumcised, why didn't He create you that way?" the Roman asked one of the rabbis. "Why does He put you to the trouble of circumcision?"

The rabbi answered, "Our God wanted us to make *ourselves* more perfect by fulfilling His holy commandments as a sign of a special Brit between Him and us."

ELIJAH THE PROPHET AND BRIT MILAH

In Europe before World War II, some synagogues owned special two-seated thrones to be used for every Brit Milah. On one of the two seats, an honored friend or family member would sit, holding the baby on his lap while the Mohel did the operation. The other seat was set aside for the prophet Elijah. Such thrones are museum pieces today, but a chair is still set aside for Elijah at every Brit. (Similarly, we always place a cup of wine for Elijah on the Passover seder table.)

In the days of wicked King Ahab (ninth century B.C.E.), Elijah was concerned that the Israelites were ignoring their

A handshake is a sign of Brit in the business world.

Brit with God. To prove to the prophet that Jews do honor that Brit, we welcome Elijah's presence each time a child is circumcised. In addition, a verse from the prophet Malachi identifies Elijah as the herald of the Mashiaḥ. Since every child is eligible to "grow up to be the Mashiaḥ," we want Elijah to meet the child at this ceremony.

After the operation has been completed, the baby's father says a prayer. In this prayer, he thanks God for commanding us to bring our sons "into the Brit of Abraham, our ancestor." The guests then say, "Even as he has now been led to the Brit, so may the child be led in due time to study, to marriage, and to good deeds." Witnessing the ceremony, Elijah should be satisfied with the family's commitment not only to the Brit but also to Jewish ideals in general.

SEE FOR YOURSELF

At Genesis 17:1–22 you can read God's Brit with the Jewish people through Abraham. Elijah's concern that the Jews were ignoring their Brit with God is expressed at 1 Kings 19:10–14. The prophecy that Elijah will be the herald of the Mashiaḥ appears at Malachi 3:23.

THINK ABOUT IT

1. Explain why circumcision is considered a fitting sign for the Brit between God and Abraham.

2. What are two reasons for welcoming Elijah to every Brit Milah?

3. What do the Brit ceremony for girls and the Brit Milah for boys have in common?

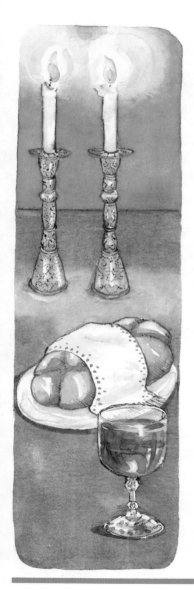

בְּרָכוֹת

BRACHOT

bə • rä • ḥôt'

Brachot means blessings. A single blessing is a Brachah (בְּרָכָה). One way to serve God is through deeds. Another way is to recite the Brachot.

Three familiar Brachot are said over wine, bread, and the Shabbat candles.

CHAPTER SEVEN

Imagine that you are driving along a tree-lined parkway. You're in such a hurry to get from one town to another that you barely notice the magnificent scenery all around you. Suddenly a sign by the roadside lets you know that an especially scenic lookout is only a mile up ahead. Slowing down, you enjoy the view of a beautiful river valley. The valley has been there all along, but without the signpost you might have missed it.

Brachot are like signposts. They help us to notice things we might otherwise overlook, and they give us the chance to appreciate things we might otherwise take for granted. Brachot also remind us that everything we experience is part of God's Creation, from daily activities like eating and drinking to once-in-a-lifetime events such as birth and death.

In this chapter, you will learn the meaning behind the Brachot. You will also read about three different types of Brachot and some examples of each that should be familiar to you.

CHAPTER SUMMARY

Lesson 1: By saying the Brachot, we ask permission to use what belongs to God.

Lesson 2: There are three main types of Brachah.

Brachot and God's temple

In ancient times, when a city was defeated and its temple destroyed, the conquered people believed that their god had lost power. They would accept the god or gods of their conquerors. But this did not happen to the Jews in 586 B.C.E., when the Babylonians destroyed the Temple in Jerusalem. Read on to understand why, and to learn how the destruction of the Temple relates to the Brachot. As you read, ask yourself:

How do the Brachot remind us that the whole world is God's Temple?

◁
Tasting the first ripe strawberries in spring—or doing anything else that feels new—is the right time to say SheHeḥeyanu.

BRACHOT PERMIT US TO USE GOD'S BELONGINGS

After the destruction of the Jerusalem Temple, the spiritual leaders of the Jews kept the people from despairing. One way these leaders did so was by teaching that God's presence was not confined to the Temple. There was only one true God, they taught, and the whole world was His Temple.

While the Jerusalem Temple stood, no one had been allowed to put any of its contents to personal use. Whoever did use a Temple object for private purposes was guilty of **sacrilege** (sak′rə•lij)—the disrespectful treatment of holy things.

Now the Jewish spiritual leaders were teaching that everything in the world was an object in God's Temple. If that were true, how could anyone be permitted to use anything without being guilty of sacrilege? The answer was by reciting a Brachah. By saying a Brachah, the Jews would show they knew they lived in God's Temple. Once they had said the Brachah, they could use whatever the world offered without fear of sacrilege.

Centuries after the destruction of the Temple, the rabbis were discussing the meaning behind the Brachot. One rabbi raised the following question: Why does one psalm say, "The earth and everything it contains belong to the Lord," while another psalm says, "The heavens are the heavens of the Lord but the earth He has given to people"? How could the earth belong to God if He has given it to people?

The Talmud answers the question in this way. Before we say a Brachah, everything on earth belongs to God. Once we say a Brachah, God gives us permission to use what His earth contains.

THINK ABOUT IT

1. In what way does saying a Brachah prevent an act of sacrilege?

2. Describe an occasion when you suddenly recognized something beautiful or exciting you had overlooked before.

HAVE YOU HEARD?

Some Brachot are said only rarely. When the Israeli writer S. Y. Agnon (1888–1970) won the Nobel Prize for literature in 1966, he was invited to Stockholm to receive his award from the King of Sweden. Despite his ill health, he decided to make the long trip in order to worship God by saying a Brachah he had never had the chance to recite before.

This Brachah was the special blessing said upon meeting a monarch: "Blessed are You, Lord our God, King of the universe, Who have given of Your glory to a human being."

The woman helping S. Y. Agnon prepare to meet the King of Sweden is Nelly Sachs (1891–1970). This German Jewish poet shared with Agnon the Nobel Prize for literature in 1966.

Three types of Brachot

In Jewish homes throughout the world, three different types of Brachot are said on the first night of many Jewish holidays. The blessing over candle lighting is one type of Brachah. The Brachot over bread and wine belong to a second type. The SheHeḥeyanu (שֶׁהֶחֱיָנוּ) Brachah is a third type. As you read more about these familiar Brachot, ask yourself:

What are the three types of Brachot most commonly said in the home?

BRACHOT FOR EVERY OCCASION

Brachot on Performing a Mitzvah You have probably known the Brachah over candle lighting for many years. We say the first ten words of that Brachah before performing many different Mitzvot:

בָּרוּךְ אַתָּה, יְיָ אֱלֹהֵינוּ, מֶלֶךְ הָעוֹלָם, אֲשֶׁר קִדְּשָׁנוּ בְּמִצְוֹתָיו וְצִוָּנוּ

These words mean: "Blessed are You, Lord our God, King of the universe, Who has made us holy through the commandments and has commanded us. . . ." Only the last words of the Brachah change. For example, during the Pesaḥ seder, we say the first ten words and add the Hebrew for "concerning the eating of matzah," עַל אֲכִילַת מַצָּה.

By saying a Brachah before lighting candles and performing other Mitzvot, we are doing several things. We thank God for giving us the opportunity to make ourselves holy through the performance of the Mitzvot. We also show that we believe the Mitzvot come from God.

Brachot for Enjoying Food and Drink Most likely, you have also known the Brachot over bread and wine for many years. Notice that only the first six words—

בָּרוּךְ אַתָּה, יְיָ אֱלֹהֵינוּ, מֶלֶךְ הָעוֹלָם

—are the same as those in the Brachah over candle lighting and the other Mitzvot. After the opening six words, the rest of the Brachah tells what God has created or done that gives us the pleasure we are about to have. Before eating bread, we say that God brought forth bread from the earth, הַמּוֹצִיא לֶחֶם מִן הָאָרֶץ. Before drinking grape juice or wine, we indicate that it was God Who created the fruit of the vine, בּוֹרֵא פְּרִי הַגָּפֶן.

You may also know some other Brachot in this category. For example, on Rosh HaShanah, before we eat apple dipped in honey, we say בּוֹרֵא פְּרִי הָעֵץ, "Who has created the fruit of the tree."

Brachot for Different Events in Our Private Lives When you receive a present on your birthday or some other special occasion, it's only right to thank the person who gave you the gift. SheHeḥeyanu is the Brachah that allows us to say thanks to God for the good things we experience in life:

בָּרוּךְ אַתָּה, יְיָ אֱלֹהֵינוּ, מֶלֶךְ הָעוֹלָם,
שֶׁהֶחֱיָנוּ וְקִיְּמָנוּ וְהִגִּיעָנוּ לַזְּמַן הַזֶּה:

The words mean: "Blessed are You, Lord our God, King of the universe, Who has kept us alive and permitted us to reach this occasion."

SheHeḥeyanu is said after candle lighting and Kiddush on the first days of holidays. Many Jews also say She-Heḥeyanu whenever they do something new, such as putting on new clothes or moving into a new home. You may also recite SheHeḥeyanu before doing something you have not done for so long it seems new, like going swimming for the first time in summer or eating the first ripe red strawberries from your own garden patch.

THINK ABOUT IT

1. How does the language of the Brachot for performing Mitzvot differ from the language of the Brachot for enjoying food and drink?

2. Describe at least one new thing you did during the past month, and at least one thing you hadn't done in so long it felt new when you did it.

SEE FOR YOURSELF

The passage in the Bible that says "everything belongs to the Lord" is Psalm 24:1. The passage that says God has given the earth to the people is Psalm 115:16.

יָמִים נוֹרָאִים

YAMIM NORAIM

yä • mēm' nô • rä • ēm'

Yamim Noraim means "Days of Awe." These are the ten days (יָמִים) beginning with Rosh HaShanah and ending with Yom Kippur.

During the Yamim Noraim we weigh the good and bad things we have done and try to find ways to do better.

CHAPTER EIGHT

The Yamim Noraim are special days on the Jewish calendar. These days are set aside for us to think about our behavior during the past year. In our prayers we ask God to forgive us for things we have done that were wrong. But tradition teaches that our prayers can win God's forgiveness only for sins we have committed against Him. If we have hurt other people, we must seek their forgiveness directly. So during the Yamim Noraim we try to improve our relationships both with other people and with God.

One year, on the afternoon before Rosh HaShanah, a man bumped into Rabbi Mordecai of Nadvorna. The rabbi recognized the man. He was a cantor.

"Why are you in such a hurry, my friend?" asked the rabbi.

"Surely you're not serious, rabbi. I have only a short time to read over the prayerbook for the Yamim Noraim—the Maḥzor. As cantor, I must put the prayers for Rosh Ha-Shanah in their proper order. That's why I'm hurrying off to the synagogue."

Rabbi Mordecai was not impressed with this answer. "Take my advice and slow down, my friend. The arrangement of prayers in the Maḥzor never changes. You'll find that the prayers for Rosh HaShanah are already in their proper order. Instead of rushing off to examine the Maḥzor, try examining what you did during the past year instead. God is more interested in your efforts to put *yourself* in proper order."

In this chapter, you will read two stories about seeking God's forgiveness during the Yamim Noraim and one story about seeking the forgiveness of other people.

◁

The shofar would not sound—and Yom Kippur could not end—until the selfish man agreed to mend his ways and care for the poor widow's children.

CHAPTER SUMMARY

Lesson 1: Forgiveness during the Yamim Noraim can be thought of as a two-way street.

Lesson 2: Seeking forgiveness from other people is just as important during the Yamim Noraim as seeking forgiveness from God.

Seeking God's forgiveness during the Yamim Noraim

The Yamim Noraim are a solemn time. But as we learn in two tales from Eastern Europe, no time of year is so solemn that it prevents someone from "talking with God" as one would with a close friend. As you read the two tales that follow, ask yourself the following question:

What kind of attitude toward God do the two rabbis and two tailors in these stories seem to share?

TWO BARGAINS WITH GOD

The first tale concerns Rabbi Levi Yitzḥak of Berditchev (c. 1740–1810). One year, during the Yamim Noraim, the rabbi brought some clothes to a tailor for mending. The rabbi was aware that the tailor did not know enough Hebrew to read the Maḥzor (מַחֲזוֹר).   He was curious to know how the tailor hoped to earn God's forgiveness on Yom Kippur, since he could not recite the prayers. But he did not want to embarrass the tailor by calling attention to his lack of education. So the rabbi asked his question in a roundabout way.

"My friend," began Rabbi Levi Yitzḥak, "each year on Yom Kippur I do much the same thing. I wonder how similar your Yom Kippur habits are to mine. How, for example, did you spend last Yom Kippur?"

The tailor answered, "I spoke up and told God the following, 'Whatever sins I have committed are very small. From time to time, I may have kept a scrap of leftover cloth instead of returning it to the person who brought me the material to make a new suit or dress. You, on the other hand, God, are guilty of some very serious sins. You have separated children from their mothers and mothers from their children. So let's make a deal: if You pardon me, I'll agree to pardon You.'"

Rabbi Levi Yitzḥak was very angry with the tailor.

"How could you do such a thing?" he scolded. "You missed a great chance. You may have earned your own for-

"To everything there is a season, and a time for every purpose under heaven; a time to be born and a time to die; a time to plant and a time to uproot what was planted; a time to kill and a time to heal; a time to tear down and a time to build up; a time to weep and a time to laugh" (Ecclesiastes 3:1—4).

giveness. But with some harder bargaining, you could have brought the Messiah."

The second story takes place on Erev Yom Kippur. Rabbi Elimelech of Lizhensk (1717—1787) sent his students to visit a tailor, telling them the tailor would teach them how to behave on the holy day. As the students approached the tailor's simple home, through the window they saw him take from a shelf what looked like two account books, one much thicker than the other. Then they heard him speak these words:

"Master of the universe, today is the day when all Jews seek Your forgiveness. And so the time has come for us to settle our account."

Then, pointing to the slimmer of the two account books, the tailor said, "In this book I have kept a list of all my sins. But look how much heavier this second account book is. In this second book I have kept a list of all the sins You committed. Look at all the pain in the world. Families are unhappy. Many people are starving, and some don't even have homes.

"Master of the universe, if we were to do a fair job of settling our account, You would owe me much more than I would owe You! But it is Erev Yom Kippur, when we are supposed to ask each other's forgiveness. For that reason, I will forgive You for Your sins if You will forgive me for mine. Let there be peace between us now."

Shocked by what they had seen, Rabbi Elimelech's students hurried back to him. They told the rabbi everything they had witnessed. They expected their teacher to share their horror at the tailor's ḥutzpah in criticizing God.

Imagine the students' surprise when Rabbi Elimelech said to them, "God Himself took great joy in the tailor's simple words."

THINK ABOUT IT

1. When you first read that Rabbi Levi Yitzḥak of Berditchev was angry at the tailor, what did you think was the reason for his anger? What was the actual reason for the rabbi's anger?

2. What was Rabbi Elimelech's real reason for sending his students to the tailor on Erev Yom Kippur?

3. Can you think of two reasons these stories became popular?

Seeking others' forgiveness during the Yamim Noraim

If you have not yet begun to fast each year on Yom Kippur, you will probably begin to do so very soon. Imagine how you will feel after the long day. You will not have eaten or drunk anything since late the previous afternoon. You will have spent much of the day in services. You will probably be hungry, thirsty, and tired. Perhaps you will also feel ready to start a new year with a clean slate. But the Yom Kippur fast cannot end until the shofar is sounded. Read about a shofar that wouldn't make a sound, and ask yourself this question:

What matters more to God: our fasts or our being kind to others?

WHY THE SHOFAR MADE NO SOUND

In a few minutes, the Yamim Noraim would be over. The long Yom Kippur fast was drawing to its end. The rabbi of one particular congregation was well known for his piety and

On the first day of Rosh HaShanah, Jews may go to a running stream or river to practice the custom of Tashlich (תַּשְׁלִיךְ), which literally means "you will cast." The worshipers say special prayers, shake their clothing, empty their pockets, and throw bread crumbs into the water to symbolize the "casting off" of sins.

good deeds. He also had a reputation for being an excellent shofar blower. But when the time came for him to blow the shofar to signal the end of Yom Kippur, not a single sound came out.

After a few moments of stunned silence, a man stepped forward. "I think I may be responsible for why the shofar wouldn't blow," he admitted.

He said that while he was walking to services that day, a poor widow had stepped from the doorway of her house and asked him to do her a favor. She said that her children had been sick since before Rosh HaShanah and that she had been unable to hear the shofar blown at all during the Yamim Noraim. She begged him to stay with her children so that she might at least hear the shofar blast that concluded Yom Kippur. But, selfishly, he had refused.

"Let me return to her house and stay with her children," he told the congregation. "As soon as she enters the sanctuary, I'm sure the rabbi will be able to sound the shofar blast."

And that is exactly what happened. Later, when the service was over, the rabbi took his shofar to the widow's home and blew a single blast for the man. "We have not done our duty during the Days of Awe if we neglect the needs of other people," the rabbi reminded him. "Seeking God's forgiveness is not enough."

THINK ABOUT IT

1. What lesson about the Yamim Noraim did the man in the story learn?

2. According to the story, what is the right relationship between prayer and good deeds?

3. Discuss an act of kindness you could perform that is like the one the man in the story finally decided to do.

4. For what sorts of behavior might you want to ask God's forgiveness?

WHAT'S YOUR OPINION?

Yom Kippur is sometimes called Yom HaKippurim. One reason given for the plural is that God needs our pardon just as much as we need God's. In what way, do you think, could God be said to "need" our pardon? What kinds of "sins" might God be charged with committing? What does the idea that God needs our pardon show about how people view God's behavior and responsibility?

KAVANAH

kä • vä • nä′

Kavanah means intention. It also suggests concentration. Worshiping with Kavanah means not saying the words of a prayer mechanically but concentrating on them and their meaning. No one can force you to do things with Kavanah, but you can learn how to put Kavanah into your actions.

Reading Torah brings an intense feeling of Kavanah.

CHAPTER NINE

Have you ever practiced for a piano recital or trained for a sports event? Your teacher or coach probably has taught you the value of concentration for excelling in these events. If you become distracted while playing, you cannot give your whole self to your performance. The difference between a good performance and an outstanding one often has to do with the performer's level of concentration.

In a similar way, Kavanah can make a real difference in our lives as Jews. Just reciting words of blessings or prayers doesn't bring people closer to God. We have to focus our thoughts on what we are saying and really mean each word we say. Judaism asks that we worship God not with words only but with the heart.

In this chapter, you will read some stories that show how concentration and intention both play important parts in worshiping with Kavanah. The second section gives some advice on how to increase the Kavanah in your own praying.

CHAPTER SUMMARY

Lesson 1: Worshiping with Kavanah involves both concentration and intention.

Lesson 2: There are different ways to increase our Kavanah while praying.

Combining concentration and intention

More than 200 years ago, the Ḥasidic movement was begun by a man known as the Baal Shem Tov (c. 1700–1760). The Baal Shem Tov taught that a Jew does not need to be learned in order to communicate with God. What is required is a combination of concentration and intention—in short, Kavanah. Many Ḥasidic stories demonstrate the importance of these two aspects of Kavanah in prayer. As you read two such stories, look for answers to these questions:

(a) What effect can wandering thoughts have on prayer?
(b) Why are uneducated Jews the central characters in so many Ḥasidic stories about prayer?

WANDERING THOUGHTS KEEP US FROM PRAYING WITH KAVANAH

The Jews of Berditchev had just finished saying the Amidah one morning. Their leader, Rabbi Levi Yitzḥak, walked over to a group of worshipers. To their surprise, he greeted them with the words that are normally addressed to guests or to people newly returned to town—"Shalom Aleichem."

"Rabbi," said the worshipers, "we have been here all morning praying with you in the same room. Why are you talking to us as if we were newcomers?"

The rabbi answered: "As soon as I finished saying the Amidah myself, I happened to look over in your direction. You were still saying the words of the prayer, but from the looks on your faces as you prayed, I could tell your thoughts were miles away—perhaps in the grain market in Odessa or the wool market in Lodz. Now that I am welcoming you home from your long business trips, I hope you can pray with a little more Kavanah."

INTENTION IS AN IMPORTANT PART OF KAVANAH

Every Rosh HaShanah, Rabbi Levi Yitzḥak told this story to his followers in the town of Berditchev:

"Once I had to stay overnight at an inn away from home. Also staying at the inn were many Jews who had come on business. In the morning, I joined the prayers of the other Jews. To my dismay, the merchants' prayers sounded like a baby's babbling. It seemed to me that all their words were either swallowed or pronounced badly.

"At the end of the service, before the merchants left on their business, I thought I would teach them a lesson by speaking in nonsense syllables like a baby: 'Goo goo ba ba.'

"When the merchants looked at me with surprise, wondering if I were a madman, I explained myself: 'The way I just sounded to you is the way you must have sounded to God. Shame on you!'

"One of the merchants then spoke up, 'You were wrong to make fun of Jews who never had the chance to learn Hebrew properly. But you were right to compare our language

In music as in prayer, the ability to avoid distraction can mean the difference between a routine performance and a great one.

to that of a baby. A baby's parents understand what its nonsense syllables mean, even if no one else does. And I'm sure God understands our prayers, and knows we spoke them with Kavanah, even if you don't.'

"How right this merchant was to put me in my place! I remind you of his words today, on Rosh HaShanah, my friends," said Levi Yitzḥak, "to reassure you that your prayers will be accepted. When people address their prayers to God with love and Kavanah, God understands them, whether or not they pronounce the words correctly."

THINK ABOUT IT

1. Which of the two stories about Levi Yitzḥak shows that concentration is an aspect of Kavanah? Which story shows that intention is another important aspect?

2. If the merchants in the second story had had the chance to learn how to pray properly, do you think the Baal Shem Tov would have told them not to bother to learn? Explain your answer.

3. How can silent prayer be related to Kavanah?

Praying with Kavanah

Praying with Kavanah all the time is not easy for anyone. But there are different methods of increasing the Kavanah in our prayers. As you read about some of these methods, ask yourself:

How can I pray with more Kavanah?

STUDY, MUSIC, AND MOVEMENT CAN INCREASE KAVANAH

One good way to increase the Kavanah in your prayers is to make sure you understand the words you are saying. Start by choosing a prayer you are familiar with but don't really understand. Think about what the prayers might mean to different people in different situations. Retell the prayer in your own words and compare your "translation" with one that your rabbi or teacher suggests.

Once you are satisfied that you understand what the words of the prayer mean, review the prayer both in Hebrew and in your English translation. You have now made the

Athletes need something like Kavanah to make the fullest use of their physical powers.

prayer your own personal prayer. If you repeat this process with other prayers, little by little you will add to your storehouse of prayers. Now that you have made the prayers more meaningful to you, you should be able to say them with conviction, or real feeling. If we can pray with conviction, it sometimes makes it easier for us to act with conviction.

Another way to make a prayer your own is to learn a melody to sing it to. A Hebrew word for a tune that may be used in worship is **Niggun,** נִגּוּן (plural נִגּוּנִים). There are often several different Niggunim to choose from. Sometimes they contrast with the **Nusaḥ** (נוּסָח), the most commonly accepted melody. You might also try setting a prayer to a new Niggun. For example, you might borrow the tune of a favorite folk song or popular song and sing the words of the prayer to it.

Other traditional ways of increasing Kavanah involve the gestures we make during prayer. For example, on Yom Kippur you may have noticed that during the confessional prayer **Ashamnu** (אָשַׁמְנוּ), some people tap themselves with their fists over their hearts. By doing so, they are expressing in action as well as words their regret for having been less than perfect during the year.

But you don't have to wait until Yom Kippur to add Kavanah to your prayers by emphasizing your words with gestures. Many Jews close their eyes tightly or cover their eyes with their hands every time they say the Shema. They do so to keep out distracting sights and thoughts that would prevent them from concentrating fully on the meaning of the prayer.

Many Jews also perform certain gestures while saying the Amidah as a way of strengthening Kavanah. They begin the Amidah by taking three steps backward—leaving their everyday world—and then three steps forward—entering God's world. Just as one would bow when entering a king's throne room, many Jews bow as they begin the first two blessings of the Amidah. At the very end of the Amidah, they take three steps backward as if they were taking leave of God once more.

Just moving your feet in certain ways isn't guaranteed to make your prayer more meaningful, of course. Automatic

HAVE YOU HEARD?

Some familiar Niggunim may have begun as tavern songs or in other unlikely places. They were adapted for prayer after they became folk melodies.

"Then shall all the trees of the forest shout for joy at the presence of the Lord" (Psalm 96:12—13).

movements may not have any more Kavanah behind them than automatically spoken words. There is no secret formula for praying with Kavanah. But next time you feel fidgety during services that seem to go on forever, it may help you to know that other Jews have shared the same feeling. One sage offered the following advice: "Make every effort to pray from the heart. Even if you do not succeed, the effort is precious in God's eyes."

THINK ABOUT IT

1. Think of a prayer to which you know more than one Niggun. Which melody helps you sing with the most Kavanah?

2. What are some of the things that tend to distract you when you are trying to pray? List three things that sometimes distract you when you are performing an errand or chore.

3. For discussion: "A good thing accomplished unintentionally is as worthy as a deed accomplished with Kavanah."

WHAT'S YOUR OPINION?

The rabbis of the Talmud taught: If your mind isn't quiet, you shouldn't pray; purify your heart before praying, and say a new prayer every day. The Baal Shem Tov told his followers that the struggle to keep unholy thoughts from disturbing our prayers and studies is never-ending. Every Jew must wage a lifetime battle to try to pray, study, and act with Kavanah.

מִדַּת הַדִּין, מִדַּת הָרַחֲמִים

MIDAT HADIN, MIDAT HARAḤAMIM

mi • dät' hä • dēn',
mi • dät' hä-rä • ḥa • mēm'

Midat HaDin means God's quality of justice. **Midat HaRaḥamim** means His quality of mercy. The world needs both Midat HaDin and Midat HaRaḥamim.

Just as mixing ice water and hot water keeps the glass from cracking, so God's mixture of justice and mercy keeps the world whole.

CHAPTER TEN

In the first chapter of the book of Genesis, the Hebrew word used for God is Elohim (אֱלֹהִים). Throughout most of the second chapter, God is called Adonai Elohim (יהוה אֱלֹהִים). The rabbis, who felt that every word in the Torah had a special meaning, gave a different interpretation for each name. Elohim, they said, represented God's quality of judgment, Midat HaDin, while Adonai represented His quality of mercy, Midat HaRaḥamim.

In this chapter, you will learn how the rabbis explained the Torah's use of different names for God in talking about Creation. The second section describes the rabbis' belief that God often allows Midat HaRaḥamim to overrule Midat HaDin. The third section teaches that human beings, who depend on Midat HaRaḥamim, are expected to model themselves on God and show mercy to one another.

CHAPTER SUMMARY

Lesson 1: Midat HaDin and Midat HaRaḥamim are both necessary if the world is to endure.

Lesson 2: The rabbis emphasized Midat HaRaḥamim over Midat HaDin.

Lesson 3: When the rabbis asked people to model themselves on God, they usually had Midat HaRaḥamim in mind.

The world needs both Midat HaDin and Midat HaRaḥamim

◁

Finding the right blend of discipline and love is a challenge for every parent.

Can parents raise children successfully by being strict judges of their behavior all the time, without ever giving in? On the other hand, how would children turn out if their parents never enforced discipline and always let them have their way? You need both discipline and love, just as your parents did when they were children. As you read a Midrash that describes how the world needs both Midat HaDin and Midat HaRaḥamim, ask yourself:

Why did the rabbis compare the world to an empty glass?

HOW TO KEEP A GLASS—AND THE WORLD—WHOLE

The rabbis asked why the second chapter of Genesis says "Adonai Elohim made earth and heaven." Why, they wondered, did the Torah use two names for God, יהוה and אֱלֹהִים.   They answered by saying that God had two qualities: Midat HaDin and Midat HaRaḥamim.

The rabbis compared the situation to that of a king who had an empty glass. "If I pour boiling water into the glass," said the king, "the glass will surely burst. If I pour ice water into it, the glass will crack."

What did the king do? He mixed the boiling water with the ice water and poured the mixture into the glass. The glass did not burst or crack.

In the same way, said the rabbis, God debated with Himself about how best to create an enduring world. "If I create the world only on the basis of mercy (רַחֲמִים), then people will see no reason to refrain from sinning. They will lie, cheat, steal, and kill each other, and the world will surely be destroyed before long. But if I am always going to judge everyone on the basis of strict justice, then I am afraid that there will soon be no people left, because every misdeed would have to be severely punished.

"For that reason I will create the world by combining Midat HaDin with Midat HaRaḥamim. I will give people both rules to live by and the freedom to seek forgiveness when they do wrong."

THINK ABOUT IT

1. How did the rabbis explain the Torah's use of two names for God in the phrase "Adonai Elohim made earth and heaven"?

2. To what did the rabbis compare the boiling water and the ice water in the story about the king?

3. Describe your parents' style of raising children. Do they emphasize Midat HaDin or Midat HaRaḥamim? Which mixture will you prefer when you are a babysitter, a camp counselor, and a parent?

Tilting the balance in favor of Midat HaRahamim

The rabbis of the Talmud had no doubt that God preferred Midhat HaRahamim to Midat HaDin. In one passage in the Talmud, they even described God as praying to Himself: "May it be My will that My mercy may overcome My anger, and that My mercy may conquer all My other qualities, so that I may deal with My children with Midat HaRahamim and for their sake not demand strict justice." Read how rabbis over

The Talmud says that when the Egyptians drowned in the Red Sea, God stopped the angels from singing.

the ages have stressed God's Midat HaRaḥamim, and ask yourself:

(a) *How did the rabbis dramatize God's preference for Midat HaRaḥamim?*
(b) *According to Rabbi Pinḥas Shapiro of Koretz, why do even sinners please God?*

GOD TAKES NO PLEASURE IN MIDAT HADIN

According to the Talmud, God gives much greater weight to the good in a person than to the bad. The rabbis expressed this attitude in a colorful way. If 999 angels testify against a person and only one angel testifies on that person's behalf, God shows Midat HaRaḥamim. And even if 999 parts of that angel's testimony are negative, and only one part casts that person in a positive light, God still chooses Midat HaRaḥamim.

When God does have to show Midat HaDin, He takes no enjoyment from it. Sometimes, when punishing a child, a parent says, "This hurts me more than it hurts you." The rabbis described God as sharing that feeling. God took no pleasure, for example, in punishing the Egyptians at the time

Showing kindness to animals is a way to imitate God's Midat HaRaḥamim.

of the Exodus. According to the Talmud, the angels began to sing God's praises as the waters of the Red Sea covered the Egyptians. God silenced the angels by saying, "My creatures lie drowned in the sea. How can you sing hymns to Me?"

EVEN SINNERS PLEASE GOD

Pinhas Shapiro of Koretz (1726—1791) was a rabbi who lived in Eastern Europe. Like the rabbis of the Talmud, he taught that God prefers Midat HaRahamim to Midat HaDin.

"If people did not sin," said Rabbi Shapiro, "God would have no occasion to use Midat HaRahamim. We can see from this fact that even sinners must please God, because they give Him the chance to show His best quality."

THINK ABOUT IT

1. How did the rabbis dramatize their belief that God is saddened when He must show Midat HaDin?

2. Describe two situations when you feel it would be right for a parent to show less Midat HaRahamim and more Midat HaDin.

3. The rabbis felt that God must have been unhappy when the Egyptians were killed. Would they have felt this way about any enemy of Israel—for example, Nazi war criminals? Why or why not?

Midat HaRahamim as a model for human behavior

When the rabbis of the Talmud teach that people should model their behavior on God's, what they have in mind is Midat HaRahamim. Read a famous story about a rabbi and Midat HaRahamim, and ask yourself:

How did Rabbi Levi Yitzhak get the official last name "Merciful"?

HAVE YOU HEARD?

Another way to imitate God's Midat HaRahamim is to show kindness to animals. Many laws in the Torah forbid treating animals cruelly. In the Book of Jonah, which is read on Yom Kippur, God tells the prophet that one reason for His not destroying Nineveh, despite the wickedness of its people, was the fact that many animals lived there. The rabbis taught that the SheHeheyanu blessing should never be said before slaughtering an animal or putting on new leather shoes, because the enjoyment of the meat or the shoes came at the cost of the animal's life.

RABBI LEVI YITZHAK "MERCIFUL"

In the official government registry, Levi Yitzhak of Berditchev's last name was given as "Merciful," even though his father was not known by that name. What led the government to register such an odd name for the rabbi?

The story goes that the king issued a decree requiring an official listing of a first name and a last name for each of his subjects. The Jews did not register themselves, so the sheriff of Berditchev went from house to house to put the new law into effect.

When the sheriff came to Levi Yitzhak's home, he reeled off his official request. But the rabbi ignored the question. Instead, looking straight into the sheriff's eyes, man to man, he said, "Try to imitate the qualities of God. As He is merciful, so you too shall be merciful."

The sheriff heard only the rabbi's last word. He removed his official list from his pocket, and wrote down: "First name, Levi Yitzhak. Second name, Merciful."

THINK ABOUT IT

1. What point was Rabbi Levi Yitzhak trying to make to the sheriff? Why did the sheriff ignore the rabbi's point?

2. Can you think of a reason why the rabbis, while opposing cruelty to animals, did not outlaw the slaughtering of cattle for leather and meat?

3. Describe a time when someone showed you Rahamim and another time when you showed Rahamim to an animal.

SEE FOR YOURSELF

God's prayer for Midat HaRahamim to overcome Midat HaDin appears in the Talmud at Brachot 7a.

מָשִׁיחַ

MASHIAH

mä • shē'äḥ

Mashiah is the Hebrew word for the Messiah. The word מָשִׁיחַ, which literally means "anointed one," is related to מָשַׁח, which means "to anoint with holy oil." Jewish tradition connects the idea of Mashiah with a future age of peace.

Jewish tradition looks forward to the end of time, when the Mashiah will bring peace and perfection.

CHAPTER ELEVEN

Every person has longings and hopes for the future. Some of these hopes have to do only with our own lives. Others have to do with the future of the world. Often, when we are feeling down, what keeps us going is the belief that things will get better, that some of these hopes will become reality.

A Jewish tradition connects Shabbat with our hopes for a better future. Many Jews observe the end of Shabbat on Saturday evening with the ceremony of Havdalah (הַבְדָּלָה). The twisted candle, the wine, and the beautiful spice box all play a part in the Havdalah ceremony. During or after the ceremony we sing a song about the prophet Elijah, Eliahu HaNavi (אֵלִיָּהוּ הַנָּבִיא). According to Jewish tradition, in the future, Eliahu HaNavi will tell the world that the Mashiaḥ is about to come, bringing a time of peace and plenty for all the world. On Shabbat, we have a taste of what that future time of peace will be like.

In this chapter, you will learn more about the time of the Mashiaḥ. You will also learn that people are partners with God—even when it comes to bringing the Mashiaḥ.

CHAPTER SUMMARY

Lesson 1: According to tradition, the days of the Mashiaḥ will be a time of peace and plenty for all people.

Lesson 2: We can help bring about the days of the Mashiaḥ by seeking good for all people.

◁

"The wolf and the lamb shall graze together, and the lion shall eat straw like the ox, and the serpent's food shall be earth. In all My sacred mount nothing evil or vile shall be done" (Isaiah 65:25).

The days of the Mashiaḥ

What has belief in the coming of the Mashiaḥ meant to Jews who have suffered? What can it mean to you? Read more about Jewish hopes for the days of the Mashiaḥ, and ask yourself:

According to tradition, how will life be different for all people in the time of the Mashiaḥ?

Anne Frank
(1929–45)

WHAT'S YOUR OPINION?

In July 1944, only a month before she and her family were captured by the Nazis, Anne Frank wrote in her diary: "I see the world gradually being turned into a wilderness. I hear the ever-approaching thunder, which will destroy us too. I can feel the sufferings of millions. And yet, if I look up into the heavens, I think that it will all come right, that this cruelty too will end, and that peace and tranquillity will return again."

A TIME OF PEACE FOR ALL PEOPLE

Jewish tradition frames life with two Golden Ages: the Garden of Eden (גַּן עֵדֶן) at the beginning of time, and the days of the Mashiaḥ (יְמוֹת הַמָּשִׁיחַ) at the end of time. In between these two Golden Ages, life as we know it goes on.

According to tradition, the days of the Mashiaḥ will bring peace. Jews and non-Jews will live in harmony. Everyone will finally understand that all people are brothers and sisters.

Have you ever tried to explain something to your parents without much success? When they finally caught on, you may have gotten a small taste of what the days of the Mashiaḥ are supposed to be like. In the days of the Mashiaḥ, parents and children will understand one another completely!

These aren't the only changes that will take place during Yemot HaMashiaḥ. The rest of nature will also become peaceful. Strong animals will no longer prey on weak ones. This is the kind of world the prophet Isaiah foresaw:

The wolf shall dwell with the lamb,
The leopard lie down with the goat.

People and animals will not have to compete for the good things on earth, because there will be enough to go around. Hunger will be a thing of the past. Everyone will be able to live in comfort. No one will be deprived of freedom, and everyone will be treated fairly.

Instead of wasting their energy in arguments and wars, all people will devote themselves to the knowledge of God. People everywhere will accept God as ruler.

What does this description of Yemot HaMashiah really mean? The belief in a future world of peace and plenty means that Jews never lose hope. No matter what suffering goes on in the world, Jews always have hope that people can be good and that the future can be better for everyone. If things seem bad, don't give up! Do your best to improve the situation, because the world can be made better.

THINK ABOUT IT

1. What are three differences between life now and in the time of the Mashiah?

2. Does the idea of Mashiah show that Judaism is an optimistic religion? Explain your answer.

3. Imagine a day in Yemot HaMashiah. Describe it through pictures, words, or music.

HAVE YOU HEARD?

The Greek word for Mashiah is *Christos*. Christians call Jesus "Christ" because they believe he is the Mashiah. Jews, however, cannot believe the Mashiah has come because, unfortunately, the age of peace we associate with the Mashiah has not yet arrived.

Waiting for the Mashiah

The rabbis of the Talmud were studying God's words to the prophet Isaiah about the days of the Mashiah. In one sentence, God seemed to be saying two different things about the Mashiah's arrival. First God said that the Mashiah would come "at the time that is set." Next God said, "I the Lord will speed up that time." If the time for the Mashiah's arrival had already been set, why did God say He would speed it up? Rabbi Joshua ben Levi (third century C.E.) explained God's words in this way: If people act properly, God will speed up the Mashiaḥ's arrival. If people do not act properly, the Mashiaḥ will come at the time that is set. As you read more about Rabbi Joshua ben Levi and the Mashiaḥ, ask yourself:

When will the Mashiaḥ come?

THE MASHIAḤ IS READY WHEN WE ARE

A legend says that Rabbi Joshua ben Levi once met Eliahu HaNavi. The rabbi knew that Eliahu's job was to announce the arrival of the Mashiaḥ. So the rabbi asked the prophet, "When will the Mashiaḥ come?"

To the rabbi's surprise, Eliahu said, "Why ask me? Go directly to the Mashiaḥ and ask him."

"But where will I find the Mashiaḥ?" asked Rabbi Joshua.

"At the gates of the town," answered Eliahu.

So Rabbi Joshua ben Levi went to the gates of the town, and found the Mashiaḥ sitting there.

"My master and teacher," said the rabbi, "when will you come?"

The Mashiaḥ answered, "Today."

Imagine how Rabbi Joshua ben Levi felt when, at the end of the day, the Mashiaḥ still had not arrived. In his disappointment, the rabbi went looking again for Eliahu HaNavi. When he found the prophet, the rabbi said, "The Mashiaḥ lied to me. He said he would come today, but he didn't."

Eliahu explained the situation to the rabbi. "The Mashiaḥ was quoting from the Book of Psalms, where it says, 'Today—if you listen to His voice.' What he meant was that people can't just sit around waiting for the Mashiaḥ to solve all their problems. They have to do their best to bring about a better world."

THINK ABOUT IT

1. According to the Talmud, what would make the Mashiaḥ come ahead of schedule?

2. In the story, what did the Mashiaḥ really mean when he told Rabbi Joshua ben Levi he would come "today"?

3. Describe two ways you can help bring about "the days of the Mashiaḥ."

WHAT'S YOUR OPINION?

In the Bible, the Hebrew word מָשִׁיחַ refers to someone who has been anointed, or made holy, by being touched with a special oil. An "anointed one" was usually a king or a high priest. Many Jews still believe that the Mashiaḥ will be like a king, reestablishing and ruling over the kingdom of Israel. Other Jews think of Mashiaḥ not as a person but as a future age of peace and perfection. We can all work to achieve a better future whether we believe in a personal Mashiaḥ or not.

נְשָׁמָה

NESHAMAH

nə • shä • mä′

Neshamah is one of the Hebrew words for soul. It is related to the word that means to breathe, נָשַׁם. The Bible says the first human being was dust until God breathed into him the breath of life, נִשְׁמַת חַיִּים. Then he became a living soul.

According to legend, smelling Havdalah spices consoles us for the loss of the extra Neshamah that leaves when Shabbat ends.

CHAPTER TWELVE

During the Havdalah ceremony we pass around a special box, often shaped like a castle, that holds sweet-smelling spices. A legend teaches us that the spices play a role in maintaining the Jewish Neshamah.

According to the legend, we Jews are given an extra Neshamah on Shabbat eve. This extra Neshamah stays with us throughout the day of rest, enabling us to put aside our routine cares and concentrate on the joys of Shabbat. When Shabbat is over, the extra Neshamah leaves, too.

The Jewish custom of smelling spices is meant to help the everyday Neshamah get over its grief at the departure of the extra Shabbat Neshamah. In a similar way, smelling salts can help revive a faint person.

In this chapter, you will find out more about the everyday Neshamah of the Jew. You will learn that Jewish tradition considers the body and the Neshamah to be equal partners in whatever bad or good things we may do.

CHAPTER SUMMARY

Lesson 1: The Neshamah and the body are equal partners.

Lesson 2: If we want to serve God with our entire Neshamah, we must keep our bodies healthy.

The Neshamah and the body are equal partners

Imagine that you are training for a sport and are supposed to be on a diet. All your friends are going out for hot fudge sundaes. You struggle with yourself but finally decide to give in and have a sundae, too. You might say to yourself, "My Neshamah wanted to be on this diet, but my body just wouldn't cooperate." Jewish tradition doesn't contrast the Neshamah and the body in this way, however. After you read the following Midrash, you should be able to answer this question:

How does the Midrash teach that the Neshamah and the body share responsibility?

SEE FOR YOURSELF

At Genesis 2:7 you can read how God transformed the first human being from dust into a living soul.

◁
The Neshamah and the body are equally responsible for the good and bad things we do.

THE NESHAMAH SHARES THE BODY'S RESPONSIBILITY

A man once came to Rabbi Yehudah HaNasi (c. second century C.E.) with the following thought: "Rabbi, after a person's death the body and the Neshamah can both claim to be free from guilt for whatever misdeeds the person committed. The body can say, 'Obviously the Neshamah is the guilty party. From the day it left me, I have been lying quietly in the grave like a stone.' And the Neshamah can say, 'Obviously the body is the guilty party. From the day I left it, I have been flying about in the air like an innocent bird.' "

Rabbi Yehudah HaNasi answered him with a story.

There was once a king who had a magnificent orchard. To protect the fruit, the king hired two guards. One of them was blind, the other lame.

After a time, both guards got hungry. The lame man told the blind man all about the fruit that hung invitingly on the trees. "Unfortunately," said the lame man, "I can't walk over to them, so I don't have any way to pick the fruit."

The blind man said, "If only I could see where the fruit hangs, I could pick some for us."

Together the two guards hatched a scheme. The lame man managed to climb onto the blind man's shoulders. Following the lame man's instructions, the blind man carried the lame man over to a fruit tree. The lame man then reached up and picked several armfuls of fruit, which the two guards shared.

Later that day, the king visited the orchard and noticed that one of his trees was almost bare. He asked the guards, "What happened to all the fruit on that tree?"

Both guards claimed innocence. "Clearly I'm unable to walk over to the tree," said the lame man. Said the blind man, "I can't even see which tree you're talking about." But the king was not taken in. He hoisted the lame man onto the back of the blind man and showed how they could have helped each other. Then the king made them stand trial together.

"In the same way, my friend," said Rabbi Yehudah HaNasi, "God considers each person's body and Neshamah as a single unit, with both parts equally responsible for whatever bad things or good things we do."

WHAT'S YOUR OPINION?

An old Jewish proverb says: "Those who find a difference between soul and body have neither."

The blind guard and the lame guard both claimed innocence, but the king knew they shared the guilt for stealing the fruit from his orchard.

THINK ABOUT IT

1. According to the story, who or what is responsible for the bad things or good things we do?

2. Contrast the Christian saying "The spirit is willing, but the flesh is weak" with the Jewish attitude toward the relationship of the body and the Neshamah.

3. Do you think that Rabbi Yehudah's story makes his point effectively? Why or why not?

A strong Neshamah in a healthy body

Just as the Neshamah and the body are equal partners in our misdeeds, they can both work together to help us do good. In fact, we must treat our bodies well so that we will be able to carry out our souls' good intentions. The Baal Shem Tov once said, "You may be free from sin, but if your body is not strong, your Neshamah will be too weak to serve God properly. If you are not strong and healthy, you will not be able to fulfill many Mitzvot." Read more about the Jewish attitude toward a strong Neshamah in a healthy body, and ask yourself:

How is the Neshamah affected if we neglect our bodies?

REFRESHING THE NESHAMAH

A student once told his teacher he felt he was ready to become a rabbi.

"What have you done to make you feel you are qualified?" asked the teacher.

"I have controlled my body," said the student proudly. "I sleep only a few hours a night and always on the ground, never on a bed. I eat nothing but grass. And I have myself whipped three times a day."

To the student's surprise, his teacher was not at all impressed.

"Young man," said the teacher, "a rabbi must understand that time spent on eating and sleeping is not wasted. The Neshamah within us refreshes itself during meals and rests during sleep. Only by keeping your body healthy can you be sure your Neshamah will be able to serve God properly."

The student's mouth fell open in amazement when the teacher concluded by saying, "At this time, young man, you may be qualified to be a donkey, but you are certainly not ready to be a rabbi."

Rest and good eating habits refresh your Neshamah as they keep your body healthy.

THINK ABOUT IT

1. Why did the teacher think the young man was more qualified to be a donkey than a rabbi?

2. A rabbi once said, "Take care of your own soul and of another man's body, but not of your own body and of another man's soul." What did he mean? How do you think the Baal Shem Tov would have responded to this remark?

עוֹלָם הַזֶּה, עוֹלָם הַבָּא

OLAM HAZEH, OLAM HABA

ō•läm′ hä•ze′, ō•läm′ hä•bä′

Olam HaZeh means this world, or our present life on earth. **Olam HaBa** means the world to come.

We live in Olam HaZeh; we wonder about Olam HaBa.

CHAPTER THIRTEEN

The idea of Olam HaBa has been very powerful for many Jews throughout Jewish history. Because nobody has ever died and then given an eyewitness account of exactly what happens after death, the rabbis wisely did not describe Olam HaBa in only one way. Instead, they offered many descriptions of what Olam HaBa might be like, each expressing an important Jewish value.

Today, some Jews no longer believe in the idea of an afterlife. Still, the notion of Olam HaBa continues to excite our hope and sense of wonder. After all, who really knows?

In this chapter you will read some stories that show how belief in Olam HaBa gave Jews confidence in God's justice and increased their commitment to improve Olam HaZeh. In the first section you will read how Rabbi Akiba's belief in Olam HaBa helped him face life's painful moments. You will also read a story that shows how belief in Olam HaBa inspired another rabbi to do good deeds in Olam HaZeh.

CHAPTER SUMMARY

Lesson 1: Rabbi Akiba's belief in Olam HaBa helped him deal with tragedy.
Lesson 2: Hopes for Olam HaBa can influence a Jew's behavior in Olam HaZeh.

Olam HaBa and the suffering of good people

A belief in Olam HaZeh and Olam HaBa helped many Jews, including Rabbi Akiba, explain why good people suffered while others "got away with murder." As you read more about Rabbi Akiba, Olam HaZeh, and Olam HaBa, ask yourself:

How did belief in Olam HaZeh and Olam HaBa help Akiba explain why the wicked sometimes prosper and the righteous suffer?

◁
Many Jews thought of Olam HaZeh as a long hall leading toward a radiant Olam HaBa.

WHY RABBI AKIBA LAUGHED

Rabbi Eliezer lay on his deathbed. Along with Eliezer's other students, Rabbi Akiba came to pay a sick call.

In great pain, Rabbi Eliezer called out, "God must be very angry with me."

Hearing their teacher suffer, all the students silently wept. All, that is, except one—Rabbi Akiba. Rabbi Akiba laughed out loud.

Shocked by his behavior, the other students demanded

Even as you live life fully in Olam HaZeh, you can enjoy
Shabbat as a foretaste of Olam HaBa.

to know what Rabbi Akiba found so funny. To their amazement, he asked them why they cried.

"Surely the answer to your question is obvious," said one student. "What can we do except cry as we witness the pain our teacher's illness is causing him?"

Akiba then said, "I don't mean any disrespect, but it's his suffering that makes me feel relieved and happy. For his whole life, Rabbi Eliezer enjoyed success after success. Tragedy never struck him. I began to worry that he might already have received all of his reward in Olam HaZeh. But now I know his reward still awaits him in Olam HaBa."

THINK ABOUT IT

1. Do you think Akiba's answer convinced the other students that laughter was a proper response to Rabbi Eliezer's suffering? Why or why not?

2. How might belief in Olam HaBa help people come to terms with the fact that wicked people sometimes escape punishment in Olam HaZeh?

3. Describe a time when you tried to comfort yourself or a friend by explaining that what seemed a defeat really wasn't. If you can't think of such a time in your own life, write a brief story on the same theme.

Belief in Olam HaBa, doing good in Olam HaZeh

In the story about Rabbi Akiba you saw how a belief in Olam HaBa could help Jews deal with setbacks in Olam HaZeh. Thoughts of Olam HaBa have also led Jews to improve their behavior in Olam HaZeh. Read the following story about how one man's hopes for Olam HaBa influenced his behavior, and ask:

How was Rabbi Zusya of Hanipol's behavior affected by his hopes concerning Olam HaBa?

ZUSYA OF HANIPOL AND THE SUKKAH IN OLAM HABA

Rabbi Zusya of Hanipol lived in Eastern Europe during the eighteenth century. Every Sukkot, Rabbi Zusya woud invite ordinary people as guests to his Sukkah. His friends and colleagues couldn't understand why the rabbi invited such simple folk instead of educated people like themselves. One year, one of his friends mustered up the courage to ask the rabbi the reason.

Rabbi Zusya explained, "I am worried that when I die, the angels will question whether I am fit to enjoy Olam HaBa, where the righteous live in the Sukkah of eternal peace. In order to strengthen my case with the angels, I welcome simple people now to my Sukkah in Olam HaZeh."

THINK ABOUT IT

1. What does Rabbi Zusya's answer show about the effect of his belief in Olam HaBa?

2. Think of two reasons other than hope for Olam HaBa that might lead someone to treat all people well. Which of the reasons do you find best, and why?

3. Why do you think some modern Jews have a hard time believing in Olam HaBa as an actual place or time? Why do others believe in it?

קְדֻשָׁה

KEDUSHAH

k ə• dōō • shä′

Kedushah means holiness. It is related to the Hebrew word קָדוֹשׁ, which means not only holy but also different or set apart.

Helping others brings Kedushah into your daily life.

CHAPTER FOURTEEN

Kedushah is the name of a prayer we say during the Amidah. But more than that, Kedushah is a very powerful idea that goes back to people's deepest feelings about the difference between what is special and what is commonplace in human life.

Imagine that you are standing outdoors on a cloudless night, with all the constellations perfectly visible against the summer sky. The wonder or awe you feel as you look upward at the heavens is a kind of Kedushah.

Another kind of Kedushah reflects the intense feeling people sometimes have for places or things connected with important events in their past. Just as good friends may come to think of a particular song or picnic spot as "theirs," so certain words and places take on Kedushah because people have felt God's presence in them. The innermost room of the ancient Temple, where God's presence was felt most strongly, became known as the Holy of Holies, קֹדֶשׁ הַקֳּדָשִׁים.

Even something from everyday life can be Kedushah. A Mezuzah on the doorpost, candlesticks on Shabbat, matzah at the Passover seder—these are all treated in a special way because through them people experience God. When you go to Bet Knesset and hold a prayerbook or read from the Torah, you share their Kedushah.

This chapter begins by discussing two prayers whose names are related to the word "Kedushah." The second section explains what the concept of Kedushah has to do with the idea of being separate or different. The chapter concludes by describing two roads to Kiddush HaShem, or making God's name sacred.

CHAPTER SUMMARY

Lesson 1: Kedushah is central to Jewish prayer.

Lesson 2: Kedushah is connected to the idea of being different, set apart, or special.

Lesson 3: Jews have practiced Kiddush HaShem both in the way they lived and in the way they died.

◁
"Holy, holy, holy is the Lord of Hosts. The whole earth is full of His glory" (Isaiah 6:3).

Prayer and the language of Kedushah

For Jews, God is the source of all Kedushah. When we try to make Kedushah part of our own lives, we are also trying to get closer to God. As you read about the language of Kedushah in prayers, ask yourself:

How do our prayers show respect for God's Kedushah and our hope that we can share in that Kedushah?

KEDUSHAH, KADDISH, AND BIRCHOT HAMITZVOT

Kedushah During the Amidah, we say a prayer together that is called Kedushah. There are different versions of Kedushah, but one verse appears in all versions of the Kedushah prayer: "Holy, holy, holy is the Lord of Hosts. The whole earth is full of His glory."

קָדוֹשׁ קָדוֹשׁ קָדוֹשׁ יְיָ צְבָאוֹת, מְלֹא כָל־הָאָרֶץ כְּבוֹדוֹ.

These words appeared first in the Book of Isaiah. The prophet Isaiah had a vision in which he saw angels surrounding God in the Temple. The angels repeated these words again and again to one another. When we repeat the angels' words during the Amidah, we stand in awe of God's Kedushah as did the angels in Isaiah's vision. To increase your Kavanah in speaking these words, try closing your eyes as you say them and thinking of the most beautiful natural sight you have ever seen. The awe you feel is only a hint of what it would feel like to be in God's presence.

Kaddish Unlike Kedushah, Kaddish (קַדִּישׁ) is not a Hebrew word. It is an Aramaic word related to the Hebrew. Jews spoke Aramaic for many centuries after the destruction of the first Temple.

We say different versions of the Kaddish prayer at different times during services. The form of the Kaddish prayer familiar to most Jews is the Mourners' Kaddish.

Kaddish is not really a prayer for the dead. It is a prayer that blesses God's name despite the loss the mourner has just suffered. By rising in the presence of the congregation and saying Kaddish, mourners show they do not blame God for

SEE FOR YOURSELF

The prophet Isaiah's vision of the angels surrounding God and proclaiming His holiness appears at Isaiah 6:2–3. You can read the commandment to love others as ourselves in Leviticus 19:18. Leviticus 19:2 records God's commandment to the Children of Israel to "be holy because I am holy."

The first part of the traditional wedding ceremony is called Kiddushin. The name indicates that the husband and wife have separated themselves from other men and women and promise to be faithful to each other.

the loss of their loved one. Instead, they proclaim God's Kedushah and thereby restate their own love of God and of life.

Birchot HaMitzvot A few of the Mitzvot in the Torah concern our relationship to God, such as observing Shabbat and not worshiping idols. But most of the Mitzvot concern our relationship to other people. "Love your fellow beings as yourself" sums up this type of Mitzvah.

By giving us the Mitzvot, God gave us the opportunity to experience Kedushah. When we perform certain Mitzvot, like candle lighting, we say Birchot HaMitzvot (בִּרְכוֹת הַמִּצְוֹת), or Brachot on the performance of Mitzvot, to thank God for sharing Kedushah with us. You already know that the important words in these Brachot are

בָּרוּךְ אַתָּה, יְיָ אֱלֹהֵינוּ, מֶלֶךְ הָעוֹלָם, אֲשֶׁר קִדְּשָׁנוּ בְּמִצְוֹתָיו

"Blessed are You, Lord Our God, King of the Universe, Who has made us holy with His Mitzvot."

So God's Kedushah is not something we simply admire from far off, although we do that when we say Kedushah and Kaddish. God's Kedushah is also something we can try to imitate. In the Torah, God tells the Hebrews, "Be holy because I am holy," קְדֹשִׁים תִּהְיוּ כִּי קָדוֹשׁ אָנִי. When we say Birchot HaMitzvot we thank God for enabling us to make Kedushah part of our daily lives.

THINK ABOUT IT

1. The Mourner's Kaddish does not mention the dead. What makes it an appropriate prayer for mourners?

2. What key phrase in Birchot HaMitzvot shows our thanks to God for enabling us to experience Kedushah?

3. Describe a scene that would help you say the Kedushah prayer with real Kavanah.

Kedushah as a way of being separate

Everybody likes to feel unique, one-of-a-kind. The Hebrew word **Kadosh** (קָדוֹשׁ) is related to this human need, for Kadosh means not only holy but also separate, set apart, or distinctive. Read more about how Kedushah is related to the idea of being separate or distinct, and ask yourself:

(a) *How is the Hebrew word for part of the marriage ceremony related to the meaning of Kadosh as "set apart"?*
(b) *How can we help make Shabbat Kadosh?*
(c) *How can each person strive for Kedushah?*

SEPARATING THE HUSBAND AND WIFE FROM OTHERS

The Hebrew word for part of the marriage ceremony is **Kiddushin** (קִדּוּשִׁין). When a man and woman marry, they promise to be faithful to one another. When a Jewish man gives a wedding ring to a Jewish woman, he says, "Behold you are consecrated to me with this ring," הֲרֵי אַתְּ מְקֻדֶּשֶׁת לִי בְּטַבַּעַת זוּ. This is another way of saying, "Our marriage makes us a distinctive unit. I will not look for another partner, and neither will you."

DISTINGUISHING SHABBAT FROM WEEKDAYS

The Kiddush we say on Shabbat eve quotes from the Book of Genesis: "And God blessed the seventh day and made it Kadosh, for on it God rested from all the work of Creation." The Ten Commandments also teach us to remember and observe Shabbat "to keep it Kadosh." In keeping Shabbat Kadosh, we show how different it is from the other six days of the week.

A story from the Midrash connects the commandment to keep Shabbat Kadosh with the idea of Kiddushin. According to this story, Shabbat complained to God, "Master of the universe, everything else You have created has a mate. All the other days of the week have partners, but I am all alone." God said to Shabbat, "The Jewish people will be your mate."

"BE HOLY"

How can each of us fulfill God's commandment to "be holy"? To answer this question we must once again look to the meaning of Kadosh as distinctive, separate, or unique.

SEE FOR YOURSELF

Three famous Biblical passages that emphasize the Kedushah of Shabbat are Genesis 2:3, Exodus 20:8, and Deuteronomy 5:12.

By following the Mitzvot we can make holiness part of our everyday lives. One rabbi explained the meaning of "Be holy" in this way: "When you are weighing a pound of meat, it should weigh a pound."

This silver Kiddush cup dates from the 1700s.

The Baal Shem Tov once told his followers, "Every single one of us has unique talents. If you try to serve God by imitating someone else, you are likely to lose yourself. Always strive to be like God by developing your own unique abilities. In that way each one of us can approach holiness."

When Rabbi Zusya of Hanipol lay on his deathbed, many of his friends came to see him. They tried to cheer Zusya in his final moments by comparing him to the great figures in Jewish history. After he had been compared to Abraham, Moses, and other outstanding people, Zusya told his friends to stop.

"I am not worried that God will compare me unfavorably to Abraham or Moses, my friends," he said. "My only concern is that God will find I have not lived up to my potential as Zusya."

THINK ABOUT IT

1. Why is "Kiddushin" a fitting word for part of the marriage ceremony?

2. Give two examples of things or people that you consider holy. Explain how they are related to the definition of קָדוֹשׁ as separate, set apart, or distinctive.

Kiddush HaShem

The familiar prayer we say over wine is called Kiddush, which means sanctification, or making sacred. Jewish tradition also honors a very different kind of Kiddush: Kiddush HaShem (קְדוּשׁ הַשֵּׁם), which means making God's name sacred. Kiddush HaShem includes acts of loyalty to the Jewish people or faith. As you read more about Kiddush HaShem, ask yourself:

(a) How did Shimon ben Shetaḥ achieve Kiddush HaShem?
(b) What does dying for Kiddush HaShem mean?

CAUSING A NON-JEW TO BLESS GOD'S NAME

One day the students of Shimon ben Shetaḥ went to the market and bought a donkey from a non-Jew as a present for their teacher. On their way home, the students carefully inspected the animal. To their surprise, they found a valuable pearl in the donkey's mane.

When the students arrived at their teacher's house, they told him what they had found. "Jewish law says you can keep a non-Jew's property if you find it," they advised him. "Now you'll be rich!"

But Shimon ben Shetaḥ took a different view. "No matter what the law says, the highest standards of Jewish life say otherwise. You bought me a donkey, not a precious jewel." When Shimon ben Shetaḥ returned the jewel to the non-Jew and explained how he had gotten it, the non-Jew said, "Blessed be the God of the Jews."

DYING FOR KIDDUSH HASHEM

Not every story of Kiddush HaShem has as happy an ending as Shimon ben Shetaḥ's. Throughout history, Jewish martyrs have chosen to die rather than let God's name or the Jewish people be dishonored.

In the spring of 1190, for example, Crusaders tried to force the Jews of York to convert to Christianity. Some who refused were killed instantly; others sought refuge in the royal castle. From the castle the Jews were able to throw stones down on their attackers, but they could not resist the mob for long. Finally, when all hope seemed lost, the rabbi told them: "It is plainly the will of the God of our fathers that we die for His holy law." And so the Jews of York died together for Kiddush HaShem.

THINK ABOUT IT

1. Why do you think the non-Jew blessed God instead of blessing Shimon ben Shetaḥ?

2. How does remembering martyrs who die for Kiddush HaShem increase Kedushah?

3. Can you think of something you might do to sanctify the name of God and Judaism in the opinion of non-Jews?

HAVE YOU HEARD?

Dying for Kiddush HaShem is not a thing of the distant past. Six million European Jews died at the hands of the Nazis during World War II. We honor those tragic victims as heroes who died for Kiddush HaShem.

SHABBAT

shä • bät′

Shabbat is the Hebrew word for the Sabbath day. The name comes from the word meaning "to rest." On the seventh day of creation, the Torah tells us, God rested, שָׁבַת.

We all take part in preparing for Shabbat.

CHAPTER FIFTEEN

A Roman officer once said to Rabbi Akiba, "What makes you think your Shabbat is any more important than the other days of the week?" Rabbi Akiba boldly answered with a question of his own: "What makes you think you are any more important than anyone else?" The officer proudly replied, "I am important because the Emperor has chosen to honor me." Said Rabbi Akiba, "That's just the way it is with Shabbat. Shabbat is more important than the other days of the week because the King of kings has chosen to honor it."

This chapter begins by explaining the origins of the Friday evening services that mark the arrival of Shabbat. You will learn why preparations for Shabbat involve everyone. The chapter ends by suggesting some ways to make Shabbat part of our lives.

CHAPTER SUMMARY

Lesson 1: The Kabbalat Shabbat service was begun by the sixteenth-century mystics of Safed in Eretz Yisrael.

Lesson 2: Get involved in preparing for Shabbat—don't leave the work for others.

Lesson 3: Shabbat can be a day of rest even in the modern world.

Kabbalat Shabbat

Between 400 and 500 years ago, many Jewish mystics moved to the town of Safed in Eretz Yisrael. For all Jews, Shabbat was the holiest day of the week. But for these mystics, each Shabbat was as holy as a wedding day. As you read about Shabbat customs in Safed, try to answer this question:

How did the mystics of Safed shape the Kabbalat Shabbat service we find in prayerbooks today?

SHABBAT IS A BRIDE

Every week, in Jewish congregations all around the world, we welcome Shabbat on Friday night in a service called **Kabbalat Shabbat** (קַבָּלַת שַׁבָּת). "Kabbalat" comes from the

---

HAVE YOU HEARD?

Of all the Jewish holidays, only Shabbat is mentioned in the Ten Commandments.

◁

Every Friday afternoon, the mystics of Safed dressed in white and went out to meet the Sabbath bride.

Hebrew word קַבֵּל, meaning "to receive." The Kabbalat Shabbat service was begun by the mystics who lived in Safed.

The mystics believed that God had both male and female qualities and that every Shabbat a holy marriage took place between these two sides of God's nature. Eventually the idea of a marriage within God was replaced by the notion that Shabbat was the bride and the Jewish people the groom.

Every Friday afternoon, the mystics of Safed dressed in white clothes. Forming a procession, they left the city and went to an open field to welcome the Shabbat bride. Along the way, they sang the six psalms that are still read at the beginning of Kabbalat Shabbat services.

The mystics also sang a hymn that Rabbi Shlomo HaLevi Alkabetz (c. 1505—1584) wrote to greet the Shabbat bride. You can find the rabbi's first two names by putting together the Hebrew letters that begin each of the hymn's first eight stanzas. This hymn, **L'cha Dodi** (לְכָה דוֹדִי), remains one of the most popular Shabbat songs to this day.

THINK ABOUT IT

1. What is the connection between Shabbat and marriage? What hymn from Kabbalat Shabbat makes that connection clear?

2. Jews may not have wedding ceremonies on Shabbat. Why do you think this is so?

Pitching in to prepare for Shabbat

Like Rabbi Akiba, the other rabbis of the Talmud felt we should all honor Shabbat because God Himself had honored it. The day was so important, they felt, that everyone had a responsibility to prepare for it personally. As you learn more about how the rabbis prepared for Shabbat, ask yourself:

How did the rabbis of the Talmud show that everyone must honor Shabbat by preparing for its arrival?

HOW THE RABBIS GOT READY FOR SHABBAT

The rabbis of the Talmud insisted on preparing personally for the arrival of Shabbat. They didn't consider themselves too important to do chores in honor of such an important guest.

One rabbi, for example, used to cut the vegetables for the Friday evening meal, while another salted the fish. Rabbah and Rav Joseph used to chop wood. Rabbi Zera assumed the task of lighting the fire in his home. Rav Naḥman took over complete responsibility for putting his house in order. He went so far as to replace all the weekday utensils with special ones for Shabbat.

In the sixteenth century, Rabbi Joseph Caro (1488–1575) compiled an important guide to Jewish law and practice. This guide, the **Shulḥan Aruch** (שֻׁלְחָן עָרוּךְ), which means "Prepared Table," is still used by traditional Jews throughout the world. According to the Shulḥan Aruch, all Jews, even those with many servants, should honor Shabbat by taking part personally in preparing for its arrival.

THINK ABOUT IT

1. To what did Rabbi Akiba compare Shabbat? How did his idea of Shabbat differ from that of the mystics of Safed?

2. How could you challenge the statement that preparing for Shabbat is "woman's work"?

Creating the feeling of Shabbat

Rabbi Menaḥem Mendel of Kotzk (1787–1859) had many rebellious ideas. A story is told that late one Saturday afternoon, the Kotzker's followers came to him ready for the new week to begin. "Rabbi," they said, "it's time for Havdalah." Much to their surprise, the Kotzker refused to conduct the ceremony. "During the week," he said, "my people have to

◁

Taking time out for a walk in the country helps make Shabbat special.

work like slaves just to survive. Only on Shabbat can we feel what it really means to be free. How can I send my people back to their daily struggle? No, I will not make Havdalah. I will not let the new week begin!"

We don't know when that Shabbat really ended. But we do know that many Jews feel a great sadness when Shabbat finally ends. You already know that preparing for Shabbat is a special time and that seeing Shabbat leave is a special time. But what about Shabbat itself? As you read on, ask yourself:

How can you make your Shabbat a day that is separate from the rest of the week?

YOU AND YOUR SHABBAT

Your great-grandparents may have had white bread, fish, and chicken as special delicacies only once a week, in honor of Shabbat. But most of us are lucky enough to eat well all week. The fact is that for most American Jews today, there is no tremendous contrast between the weekdays and Shabbat. Even so, Shabbat can have a very special meaning in your life.

You can make Shabbat a weekly celebration both by not doing some weekday things and by doing some special Shabbat things. Some weekday things to avoid might include unnecessary driving and shopping. Some special Shabbat activities might include a festive family dinner, some reading of Jewish writings or singing of Jewish songs, and leisurely time for family discussion. Together with rituals like candle lighting, Havdalah, and Brachot, these Shabbat customs can help us see ourselves as God's partners in Creation.

THINK ABOUT IT

1. Why did the Kotzker refuse to make Havdalah?

2. List three ways you could increase the restfulness and Kedushah of your Shabbat observance.

WHAT'S YOUR OPINION?

Exodus 20:9 says "Six days you shall labor and do all your work." A modern rabbi wondered how we could possibly do all our work in just six days, since there is always something more to accomplish. The answer, he suggested, is that we should rest on Shabbat as though we had done everything there was to do. Then we could avoid spoiling our Shabbat rest by worrying about all the work and chores that lay ahead.

שָׁלֹשׁ רְגָלִים

SHALOSH REGALIM

shä • lôsh′ rə • gä • lēm′

The **Shalosh Regalim,** or three pilgrimage festivals, are Pesaḥ, Shavuot, and Sukkot. In ancient times, our ancestors celebrated each of these holidays by making a pilgrimage to the Temple in Jerusalem.

On the Shalosh Regalim, our ancestors made pilgrimages to the Temple in Jerusalem.

CHAPTER SIXTEEN

שָׁלֹשׁ means three. רְגָלִים comes from the word for foot, רֶגֶל. On the Shalosh Regalim, most of the pilgrims traveled to the Temple on foot. Even if they rode most of the way on the backs of animals, the pilgrims had to make the last stage of the journey on foot. They were required to walk from Jerusalem up the Temple Mount.

◁
"So long as the earth endures, seedtime and harvest, cold and heat, summer and winter, day and night shall not cease" (Genesis 8:22).

What thoughts come to your mind when you hear the words Pesaḥ, Shavuot, and Sukkot? Do you think of special holiday foods, like matzah or blintzes? Do you think of the different seasons—autumn with its winds and rains, and spring and early summer with their gentler weather? Do you think of different events in the early history of our people—the Exodus from Egypt, the giving of the Torah, the forty-year journey through the desert to Eretz Yisrael? Perhaps you think of how these holidays are celebrated at home and in Bet Knesset—the seder, confirmation ceremonies, services and meals in the Sukkah.

To our ancestors long ago, the names of the Shalosh Regalim would certainly have brought to mind the trip to Jerusalem and the service at the Temple. One ancient author claims that more than three million pilgrims made the trip to the Temple on a single Pesaḥ.

In this chapter, you will learn how each of the Shalosh Regalim enriches Jewish life. Pesaḥ, Shavuot, and Sukkot all remind us of our agricultural heritage. Each of the Shalosh Regalim also reflects important events in the history of our people.

CHAPTER SUMMARY

Lesson 1: As agricultural holidays, the Shalosh Regalim remind us that all our gifts come from God.

Lesson 2: As historical holidays, the Shalosh Regalim celebrate events that teach important moral lessons.

The Shalosh Regalim as harvest holidays

Each of the Shalosh Regalim marks a harvest season in Eretz Yisrael. The pilgrims of long ago had to do more than show up at the Temple on the Shalosh Regalim. They were required to bring with them a gift from the new harvest. In this way, they showed their thanks to God for blessing the land.

As you read more about the connection between the Shalosh Regalim and the different harvest seasons, ask yourself:

What lesson can even nonfarmers learn from the observance of the Shalosh Regalim as harvest holidays?

ALL OUR GIFTS COME FROM GOD

Pesah During the seder on the second night of Pesah (פֶּסַח), the Haggadah instructs us to "count the omer." What is the omer, and what does it mean to count it?

Pesah marks the beginning of the grain harvest in Eretz Yisrael. Our ancestors harvested the first grain crop, barley, at this time of year. On the second day of the holiday, they brought as an offering to the Temple a small amount of barley weighing exactly one omer.

From the second night of Pesah for the next seven weeks, some Jews say a special Brachah each evening. Following the Brachah they say, "This is the (first, second, and so on) day of the omer."

After the seven weeks are up, it is time to celebrate the second of the Shalosh Regalim—Shavuot, which means "weeks."

These pictures should help you remember the Shalosh Regalim. From upper left to lower right: for Pesah, a seder plate and the memory of the pyramids in Egypt; for Shavuot, the Ten Commandments and a display of first fruits; and for Sukkot, a colorfully decorated Sukkah.

Shavuot We celebrate Shavuot (שָׁבוּעוֹת) at the time of the wheat harvest in Eretz Yisrael. In the Torah, Shavuot is sometimes called Ḥag HaKatzir (חַג הַקָּצִיר), which means harvest holiday.

Another name for Shavuot in the Torah is Ḥag Ha-Bikkurim (חַג הַבִּכּוּרִים), or holiday of the first fruits. In Israel today, farmers still celebrate Shavuot by offering up their first fruits. There is no longer a Temple, of course. So instead of offering the first fruits on the Temple altar, some farmers give the money from the sale of their produce to the Jewish National Fund.

Jews around the world celebrate Shavuot in other ways that show it is a harvest holiday. We read the Book of Ruth, which describes the summer harvest in ancient Eretz Yisrael. We decorate the Bet Knesset with flowers. And in America, the confirmation ceremony that takes place in many congregations also shows that this is Ḥag HaBikkurim. Parents and teachers proudly present their children to the congregation as the "first fruits" of the Jewish community.

Sukkot On the third of the Shalosh Regalim, Sukkot (סֻכּוֹת), our Hebrew ancestors made a pilgrimage to the Temple to thank God for the fall harvest. The early American Pilgrims,

who knew the Bible very well, had Sukkot in mind when they celebrated their first successful harvest on these shores with a community feast. So the American holiday of Thanksgiving is really based on Sukkot.

Two symbols of Sukkot, the lulav (לוּלָב) and the etrog (אֶתְרוֹג), show the holiday's agricultural origins. The etrog is a citron, a citrus fruit related to the lemon. The lulav is a palm branch bound together with sprigs of myrtle and willow. In order to grow properly, the citron, palm, myrtle, and willow all need plenty of rain. At the beginning of the rainy season, on Sukkot, we hold the etrog and lulav together and wave them in all directions. This is our way of showing that even today we depend on God to send the right amount of rain at the proper time.

What lesson can the many Jews today who do not farm learn from the observance of the Shalosh Regalim as agricultural holidays? We should be reminded that not only the earth's bounty but also all our gifts and talents come from God. Just as our ancestors were obliged to offer their gifts to God, so we have an obligation to use our gifts and talents to serve God.

THINK ABOUT IT

1. To which of the Shalosh Regalim is the American Thanksgiving related?

2. Describe one way in which Shavuot is still celebrated as a harvest holiday in (a) Israel, (b) America, and (c) around the world.

3. Describe one kind of "offering" you could make on the Shalosh Regalim in place of a harvest.

The Shalosh Regalim and Jewish history

Even after the Temple was destroyed and most Jews became town and city people rather than farmers, the Shalosh Regalim retained their importance. Each holiday reminded the Jews of their special relationship to Eretz Israel. Each holi-

HAVE YOU HEARD?

A pilgrimage (pil′gra • mij) is a journey, especially to a holy place. The English Puritans who came to Massachusetts in 1620 were called Pilgrims because they made the long journey from England to the New World.

day was also a reminder of an important event in the history of our people. As you learn more about the events the Shalosh Regalim celebrate, ask yourself this question:

What lessons can we learn from the historical events the Shalosh Regalim recall?

OTHER LESSONS OF THE SHALOSH REGALIM

Pesaḥ Ever since you were old enough to pay attention at the seder, you have known what historical event Pesaḥ celebrates: the Exodus of the Hebrew slaves from Egypt. But on Pesaḥ we do more than remember one of the major events in our history. We also see in it hope for the future. Just as God freed our ancestors who were slaves in Egypt, we hope He will liberate all oppressed people everywhere. When we say "Next year in Jerusalem," for example, we may think of the Russian Jews who are forbidden to leave the Soviet Union.

A story is told about the last fighters in the Warsaw Ghetto on the first night of Pesaḥ in 1943. One of the young leaders of the hopeless struggle against the Nazis decided to hold a seder. He had no Haggadah but recited from memory as best he could. When he said, "And the Lord has freed us from the bondage of Egypt," one of his comrades protested.

"It's a lie. God never freed us from slavery. Slavery and oppression follow the Jews wherever they live."

But the leader of the group had the last word. "People are free," he said, "as long as they fight against evil."

Shavuot In the Torah, Shavuot is not connected with any historical event. But the rabbis of the Talmud figured out that our ancestors received the Torah at Mount Sinai on the same day that Shavuot is celebrated: the sixth day of the Hebrew month of Sivan. So we also call Shavuot the holiday of the giving of our Torah, זְמַן מַתַּן תּוֹרָתֵנוּ.

Many of the ways we celebrate Shavuot help us recall this greatest event in our history. For example, the heroine of the Book of Ruth accepted the Torah by converting to Judaism, just as our people accepted the Torah on Shavuot. The

Made in France during the eighteenth century, this glass and silver calendar is designed to count the omer from the second night of Pesaḥ to the first night of Shavuot.

confirmation ceremonies held on Shavuot show our continued commitment to the Torah.

Do you eagerly count the days to your birthday or to summer vacation? In the same way, by counting the omer on the days between Pesaḥ and Shavuot we share our ancestors' eagerness to receive the Torah. The counting that marks the days between the two Regalim also shows that Shavuot is really the conclusion of Pesaḥ. The lesson we learn from the connection between the two holidays is that freedom is not enough. We need the Torah to teach us how to live our lives as free people.

Sukkot The Torah emphasizes both the historical and the agricultural meanings of Sukkot. We build Sukkot, or booths, every autumn in order to recall the desert homes our ancestors lived in for forty years before entering Eretz Yisrael. Those forty years were not easy ones. What kept our ancestors going was their trust in God.

The historical events that Pesaḥ and Shavuot celebrate took place at a specific time of year. But Sukkot marks a stage that took forty years. Why, then, do we celebrate Sukkot in the autumn and not during the summer or spring, when it would be more pleasant to eat in temporary huts?

If we celebrated Sukkot in the summer or spring, we would feel so comfortable sitting in our temporary huts that we might forget about our dependence on God. But in the autumn chill, when we leave our permanent homes for a meal in the Sukkah, we remember how dependent we are on God. Without God's help, our success is no more solid than the walls of the Sukkah.

THINK ABOUT IT

1. In what way is Shavuot the conclusion of the Pesaḥ season?

2. Why is it fitting for us to celebrate Sukkot in the fall?

3. Which of the Shalosh Regalim is your favorite? Describe three things about that holiday that make it your favorite.

SHEMA

shə• mä′

Shema is short for the six words שְׁמַע יִשְׂרָאֵל: יְיָ אֱלֹהֵינוּ, יְיָ אֶחָד, which mean "Hear, O Israel, the Lord is our God, the Lord is One." The full Shema actually has three complete paragraphs.

Every Mezuzah contains the Shema.

CHAPTER SEVENTEEN

The first Hebrew words you learned may have been the six words of the Shema. By now, you are probably able to read the Shema in Hebrew, but have you ever looked closely at the special way the words of the Shema are printed in the Hebrew Bible? Notice that the ayin that ends the word שְׁמַע and the dalet that ends the word אֶחָד are printed in large letters.

Why are the ayin and the dalet singled out in this way? One reason is that together they make up the Hebrew word עֵד, which means "witness." Every time we read the Shema, the Hebrew printing reminds us that we act as witnesses to the fact that God is One.

In this chapter, you will read a story that explains the response that follows the Shema. You will also learn about some of the Mitzvot the Shema teaches.

CHAPTER SUMMARY

Lesson 1: A Midrash about Jacob and his sons uses the Shema to tell of their loyalty to God.

Lesson 2: The V'Ahavta teaches several important Mitzvot.

Israel's loyalty to God

Have your parents ever asked you to reassure them that you share their values and beliefs? According to one story, the response to the Shema is the result of such a request from our ancestor Jacob. Read an explanation of why we recite this particular response, and ask yourself this question:

How does the response to the Shema reaffirm our loyalty to God?

JACOB AND THE SHEMA

When we recite the Shema, we are repeating Moses' words to the Israelites: "Hear, O Israel, the Lord is our God, the Lord is One." After reminding the people of God's Oneness, Moses

◁
"Where were you when I laid the earth's foundations? . . . Who set its cornerstone when the morning stars sang together and all the divine beings shouted for joy?" (Job 38:4–7).

immediately instructed them to love God. When we read the paragraph that begins "V'Ahavta," we are repeating these instructions. Yet in the prayerbook, the Shema and V'Ahavta are separated by a response not found in the Torah: "Blessed is the name of His glorious Majesty forever and ever."

בָּרוּךְ שֵׁם כְּבוֹד מַלְכוּתוֹ לְעוֹלָם וָעֶד!

A story that explains why we recite these words starts with the fact that God gave our ancestor Jacob an additional name: Israel. As Israel lay on his deathbed, his twelve sons gathered around him. Israel was about to tell his sons the exact time in the future when the Mashiaḥ would come. But all of a sudden, Israel felt that God's presence was slipping away from him.

Could it be, he worried, that God was abandoning him because one of his sons had lost faith? He asked them to tell him if that were true. Instead, all twelve answered together, using the words of the Shema for the first time: "Hear, O Israel, the Lord is our God, the Lord is One."

Israel was very relieved to hear their answer. In return he said, "Blessed is the name of His glorious Majesty forever and ever."

The V'Ahavta commands us to teach God's words to our children. Because of this Mitzvah, Jews commit themselves to teaching and learning.

THINK ABOUT IT

1. To whom were Jacob's sons talking when they said, "Hear, O Israel"? Explain your answer.

2. How does this story show the importance in Judaism of teaching values to one's children?

V'Ahavta

You probably know the V'Ahavta paragraph of the Shema very well, whether in Hebrew or in English or in both languages. You may know how to chant the וְאָהַבְתָּ in Hebrew, or you may know a tune to the English translation, "You shall love the Lord your God." But you may not have thought very hard

about the different Mitzvot the paragraph teaches. Read more about the meaning of this paragraph of the Shema, and ask yourself:

How does the V'Ahavta command us to show our love for God?

SHOWING LOVE FOR GOD

The first Mitzvah in the V'Ahavta is to love God. When ancient peoples worshiped their gods, they did so out of fear, not love. But Jews consider it a Mitzvah to fulfill God's commandments out of love, not fear.

We are told to love God with all our heart, with all our soul, and with our whole being. As you know, the rabbis found meaning in every word of the Torah. Loving with the heart, with the soul, and with our whole being must mean three different things.

The word for heart in Hebrew is לֵב. Usually, the form of the word meaning "your heart" is spelled לְבְּךָ, with one ב. In the V'Ahavta paragraph, the word is spelled לְבָבְךָ, with two. Why?

According to the rabbis, all people have two warring impulses within them: an impulse to do good and an impulse to do bad. Each ב in the word לְבָבְךָ stands for one of these impulses. To love God with *all* your heart means that your love of God overpowers any urge you might feel to do evil.

The rabbis taught that to love God with all your soul means to be willing to die to keep God's name holy—to die for Kiddush HaShem. A famous story connects Rabbi Akiba's death with this part of the Shema.

Rabbi Akiba helped lead a Jewish rebellion against Roman rule. For his part in the rebellion, the Romans tortured him to death. Rabbi Akiba did not cry out with pain as he was being tortured. Instead, he recited the Shema with a smile on his face.

A Roman officer said to him, "You must be a magician, old man, to be able to smile while being tortured."

Rabbi Akiba answered, "No, I'm not a magician. Each

time I said the Shema in the past, I wondered whether I would ever be able to show my love for God with my whole soul. Now I'm smiling with joy because I've finally had the chance to do so."

OTHER MITZVOT IN THE V'AHAVTA

The V'Ahavta does more than command us to love God, however. It goes on to say several things. First, we must teach God's words to our children, וְשִׁנַּנְתָּם לְבָנֶיךָ. Because of this Mitzvah, Jews have always been concerned with education and learning.

Second, we are commanded to talk about God when we lie down and when we rise up, וּבְשָׁכְבְּךָ וּבְקוּמֶךָ. The rabbis understood this to mean that we should say the Shema before going to bed at night and when we first get up in the morning.

The V'Ahavta paragraph concludes with two more Mitzvot: the Mitzvah of wearing Tefillin and the Mitzvah of placing a Mezuzah on the doorpost. Tefillin are two small leather boxes that some male and fewer female Jews wear during weekday morning services. Inside the Tefillin are pieces of parchment inscribed with passages from the first two paragraphs of the Shema and from elsewhere in the Torah. Every Mezuzah contains a piece of parchment on which the first two paragraphs of the Shema are written.

Ancient peoples worshiped their gods out of fear, not love.

THINK ABOUT IT

1. List four Mitzvot found in the V'Ahavta paragraph of the Shema.

2. What is the relationship between these four Mitzvot and our proclaiming that God is One?

TEFILLAH

tə • fē • lä′

Tefillah means prayer. It comes from
פָּלֵל, meaning "to judge." When we pray,
we judge ourselves and call upon God to
judge us.

Tefillah challenges us to examine ourselves, so we may act in a more
Godly manner.

The verb "to pray" in Hebrew is הִתְפַּלֵּל. This word also means "to judge oneself."

Jewish congregations worship using a variety of Siddurim (סִדּוּרִים), or Jewish prayerbooks. If you attend a Bar or Bat Mitzvah in a friend's or relative's synagogue, you may find that the Siddur (סִדּוּר) used by the congregation you are visiting is different from the one you are familiar with. But the basic Tefillah service will be familiar to you, no matter which synagogue you pray in.

In this chapter, you will learn some Jewish attitudes about the purpose of Tefillah. You will also learn that prayer has some limits.

CHAPTER SUMMARY

Lesson 1: Tefillah serves different purposes for different Jews.

Lesson 2: Prayer shouldn't be used to make life difficult for others or to make your own life too easy.

Tefillah serves different purposes

Imagine that you are at a Jewish summer camp where daily morning services are part of the routine. You are reading the Amidah especially carefully this morning. All of a sudden, you come to the section where we ask God to hear our voices and where we bless God for hearing prayer. For the first time you ask yourself, "Hey, wait a minute. Do I really believe this? If God really hears prayer, why do some prayers go unanswered? Why do people die even though their loved ones pray for them to live? And if I don't believe that God answers prayer, what's the point of praying at all?"

Many Jews have asked themselves questions like these. Different Jews have different ways of dealing with the problem and different feelings about why they should continue to pray. As you read about some purposes that Tefillah serves for different Jews, ask yourself this question:

What are three different ways of understanding what Tefillah is?

◄

"I will praise You, Lord, with all my heart; I will tell all Your wonders. I will rejoice and exult in You, singing a hymn to Your name, O Most High" (Psalm 9:2–3).

TEFILLAH IS A MITZVAH

Some Jews don't feel the need to explain the point of praying. They pray because it is a Mitzvah to do so. They believe they are fulfilling an obligation by praying, just as a soldier fulfills an obligation by following the orders of a commanding officer.

According to one story, a man and his son once spent an entire Shabbat afternoon arguing whether or not God existed. The father, who knew of many unanswered prayers, argued that there was no God. The son, filled with hopes of youth, argued that the order and magnificence of the natural world proved God had to exist. After hours of arguing back and forth, the father glanced at his watch. "Son," he said, "it's time to go to synagogue for evening services. After we do that Mitzvah, we can go back to arguing about whether or not there's a God."

TEFILLAH ENABLES US TO CHANGE OURSELVES

Some Jews say Tefillah is for us, not for God. They believe that when they pray, they awaken the divine in themselves, and in that sense God hears their prayers.

How do we awaken the spark of Godliness in ourselves when we pray? Tefillah gives us the chance to examine our actions and to challenge and judge ourselves. For example, when we read the words in the Amidah that praise God for sustaining the living, we should ask ourselves whether we are doing our share to make sure people have safe places to live and enough food to eat. In the same way, when we praise God for the glories of nature, we should ask ourselves whether we are doing our part to help the environment. When we bless God as giver of knowledge, we should ask ourselves if we are using our own knowledge for worthwhile goals.

According to this view, the purpose of Tefillah is not to change God but rather to make ourselves act in a more Godly fashion. A wise person once said, "If you do not feel a sense of self-improvement after praying, then your Tefillah was in vain."

HAVE YOU HEARD?

Sometimes the word Tefillah is used to refer to the Amidah, which is the central prayer of every service.

TEFILLAH UNITES US WITH JEWS EVERYWHERE

Another helpful view of the purpose of Tefillah is that it provides a common bond with Jewish communities everywhere. If you find yourself in Rome or Paris and you do not speak a word of Italian or French, you can still go to synagogue and find that you have much in common with the Jews who are praying there.

In addition, Tefillah unites Jews today with Jewish people of the past. The prayers in the Siddur were written at different times in Jewish history. Some sections come from the Bible or some are from the Talmud; others were written by

You probably differ in many ways from these Jews of Tunisia. But if you entered this synagogue on their island of Djerba, you would find that their prayers have much in common with the ones you say in your temple back home.

poets over the centuries or even in our own time. Just as it is sometimes important to feel your uniqueness as an individual, at other times it is comforting to know you are part of a tradition and of a larger group.

THINK ABOUT IT

1. What are the three different purposes of Tefillah discussed in this section?

2. Which of these purposes means the most to you? Can you think of other purposes of prayer?

3. How would you answer the question, "Does God hear prayer?"

The limits of prayer

Siddurim make it possible for us to achieve the purposes of Tefillah. If there were no prayers available for us to read from Siddurim, we might not fulfill the Mitzvah of Tefillah. If we all wrote our own prayers, we might not push ourselves to examine our shortcomings the way we can with the fixed prayers in the Siddur. And if Jews throughout the world only prayed in a spontaneous manner, we would lose an important link that binds us into a single people.

Still, it is important to remember that many prayers in our Siddurim were once personal prayers written by Jews in response to the needs of their times. If we are to pray with Kavanah, we must also speak our own thoughts and hopes in Tefillah.

There is no simple formula for writing your own prayers, but there are some things you should know before you start. As you read more about the limits of prayer, ask yourself:

(a) Why did the Kotzker refuse a man's request for a Tefillah to make his sons study Torah?
(b) What kinds of things make improper subjects for Tefillah?

Prayer can make you a better person and can help make the world a better place, but it can't get you a good grade on a test if you neglected to study.

DON'T EXPECT TEFILLAH TO DO YOUR WORK FOR YOU

A man once came to Rabbi Menaḥem Mendel of Kotzk. He pleaded with the Kotzker to say a Tefillah asking God to make the man's sons study Torah willingly. To his surprise, the Kotzker refused.

"My friend," the rabbi explained, "you obviously don't understand what true Tefillah is. A Tefillah should not ask God to do our work for us. Every day when you say the V'Ahavta, you repeat one of the basic Mitzvot a parent must fulfill: 'And you shall teach them to your children,' וְשִׁנַּנְתָּם לְבָנֶיךָ. It is your job to teach Torah to your children.

"How can you best accomplish your goal? Not by praying for your sons to become students of Torah but by setting a good example and becoming a student of Torah yourself. Tefillah, my friend, is not meant as a way of transferring our responsibilities to God. God only helps us if we try to accomplish our goals to the best of our ability."

SELFISHNESS AND LAZINESS HAVE NO PLACE IN TEFILLAH

Suppose that tomorrow morning you're scheduled to take an extremely important exam. You fear your average will drop if you don't do well. Is there any sense in your trying to make a bargain with God like this one: "If only I pass the test and Leslie fails, I promise to give half my allowance each week to some worthwhile Tzedakah"?

Or imagine yourself sitting in a dentist's chair, waiting for X-rays to be developed and worrying about the possible discomfort involved in having your teeth filled. Is there any point to your saying, "Please God, let me have no cavities"?

Think about some of the reasons why these are not worthy prayers. In the case of the exam, it's not right to pray for someone to be worse off than you are. Moreover, if you've studied hard, you should do just fine on the test; if you haven't studied, it's wrong to ask God to bail you out. Finally, you can't bribe God with promises of giving Tzedakah. The prayer said in the dentist's chair is equally improper. Tefillah is not a way of changing conditions that already exist. You either have cavities or you don't.

Not every concern is worthy of Tefillah. Your prayers should not be selfish. You should not wish suffering on others. Don't pray for the impossible.

THINK ABOUT IT

1. How is the saying "God helps those who help themselves" related to the story of the Kotzker?

2. Make a list of some of your goals for humanity, such as wiping out hunger, injustice, and the threat of war. Try to write a worthy Tefillah that focuses on these goals.

תִּקּוּן

TIKKUN

ti • kōōn'

Tikkun means "repair" or "improvement." תִּקּוּן comes from the Hebrew verb תִּקֵן, which means "to repair." Each of us has the responsibility to help make a more perfect world.

We are God's partners in improving the world.

CHAPTER NINETEEN

In one section of the Aleinu (עָלֵינוּ) prayer, we share some of our hopes with God. We ask to be shown how "to improve the world under God," לְתַקֵּן עוֹלָם בְּמַלְכוּת שַׁדַּי. These words suggest that people have an important role to play in improving the world. When we say the Aleinu, we say to God that we look forward to a time when our efforts, together with His help and support, will bring about a more perfect world.

In this chapter, you will learn about the Jewish belief that people are God's partners in improving the world. You will also learn about the system of Tikkun the mystics of Safed developed.

CHAPTER SUMMARY

Lesson 1: People are God's partners in making this a more perfect world.

Lesson 2: The mystics of Safed taught that every fulfilled Mitzvah contributes to Tikkun.

People are God's partners in Tikkun

From early times, Jews have felt that God considers us His partners in Tikkun. As you read some stories from the days of the Talmud about people as God's partners in improving the world, ask yourself:

On what did the rabbis base their belief in the partnership between people and God?

MIDRASHIM ABOUT TIKKUN

As you might expect, the rabbis based their belief in the partnership between people and God at least partly on their reading of the Torah.

Rabbi Assi, who lived during the third century C.E., found what seemed to be a contradiction between two passages in the Book of Genesis. One passage says the earth brought forth

◁
The world as we know it is not perfect, Luria said. Through the Mitzvot, every Jew can help God by repairing the vessels that shattered at the instant of Creation.

grass on the third day of Creation. But a later sentence says there were still no shrubs on the face of the earth on the sixth day, when Adam was created. How could both sentences be true?

Rabbi Assi solved the problem by suggesting that the grass hovered on the threshold of the earth until Adam was created. Only as a result of Adam's work and prayers did the grass and shrubs take root. In other words, before God's earth could be covered with greenery as He intended it to be, some human effort was needed.

The rabbis also found evidence of the partnership between people and God as they looked around the world. They noticed that God did not create loaves of bread, for example. Instead, He created wheat, which people must plant, grow, harvest, grind into flour, mix with other ingredients, and bake into bread. The rabbis concluded that everything God made during the six days of Creation needs improvement, or Tikkun. They pointed out that this need for Tikkun applies to human beings, too.

One day, two of the rabbis, Akiba and Ishmael ben Elisha, were taking a walk together. All of a sudden they found a man lying ill alongside the road. Noticing a farmer plowing his field nearby, Rabbi Ishmael asked him to go fetch a doctor.

"What's the matter with you, rabbi?" said the farmer. "How can a God-fearing person like you see any need to call a doctor? God obviously intended for this man to be ill. If God wants him to live, he'll live. If God wants him to die, he'll die."

Rabbi Ishmael responded with a question. "What are you doing with that piece of equipment?" he asked.

The farmer answered, "Any fool can see that I'm plowing."

"What's the matter with you, farmer?" said the rabbi. "How can a God-fearing person like you see any need to plow the earth? If God wants your crops to grow, they'll grow. If God wants your crops to fail, they'll fail."

"I see your point, rabbi," said the farmer. "Just as I work as God's partner in making the earth fruitful, so the doctor is God's partner in healing the sick. I'll go look for a doctor to help this man right away."

SEE FOR YOURSELF

The two passages in Genesis that troubled Rabbi Assi are 1:11–13, which says the earth brought forth plants on the third day, and 2:5–7, which suggests that humanity was created before any grasses had sprouted in the fields.

Tikkun can mean a campaign to clean up a neighborhood or a program to provide shelter for the homeless.

THINK ABOUT IT

1. Do these Midrashim suggest that the rabbis had high hopes about people's ability to perfect the world? Explain your answer.

2. List three inventions that have helped improve the world and discuss their effects.

Isaac Luria and Tikkun

Do you remember reading about the mystics in Safed (pages 103–04) who developed the Kabbalat Shabbat ceremony? One of the most important mystics in Safed was Isaac Luria (1534–1572). Luria worked out a very detailed explanation of why there is a need for Tikkun and how each Jew has a very important part to play in repairing the world. As you read more about Luria's ideas on Tikkun, look for an answer to this question:

According to Isaac Luria, what role does performing Mitzvot play in Tikkun?

THE JEW, THE MITZVOT, AND TIKKUN

Luria began with this question: If God is all-good and all-powerful, and if He has a pact, or Brit, with Israel, why do the Jews suffer so much? Why, for example, were the Jews driven out of Spain in 1492 after having lived there for more than eight centuries?

According to Luria, the answer lies in what happened at the very moment of Creation. Before Creation, there was nothing but God. In order to make room for the world, God had to contract Himself. For a moment, God limited His own power. (In the same way, parents sometimes have to restrain themselves if they want their children to learn. Many parents, for example, teach a child not to touch a hot stove by allowing the curious child to burn a finger—briefly. It may be difficult for parents not to put out a hand to stop the child, but they know their self-restraint is for the child's own good.)

Luria explained that at Creation, it was as if God had to take a deep breath to make room for the world to exist. Then, when He breathed out again, the divine light that flowed into the world was too powerful. God had intended that the light be collected in vessels. But the light was so intense, the vessels shattered. Instead of staying where it was meant to, the light went every which way. So the world as we know it is not the world God intended to create.

According to Luria, God chose the Jews to repair the broken vessels. How could they repair them? By observing the Mitzvot. Each time a Jew fulfills a Mitzvah, part of the divine system is restored, allowing the divine light to flow into the world as God originally intended.

Furthermore, said Luria, every Jew, without knowing it, has been assigned a specific repair job. No one can perform

WHAT'S YOUR OPINION?

A wise person once claimed that modern inventions help improve human character. For example, from trains (and airplanes, although they hadn't been invented at the time this man lived) people learn that "because of one second, one can miss everything." From telephones we learn "that what we say here is heard there."

If this person were alive today, do you think he would argue that such twentieth-century inventions as television, computers, and nuclear weapons have made us better as people?

Often Tikkun means repairing the damage others have done. These young people are using straw to soak up an oil spill in San Francisco Bay.

another person's assignment. So no Jew should say, "I won't bother giving Tzedakah this week. My brother will give Tzedakah in Hebrew school, and my parents make a big contribution through their temple dues, so why should I bother?" Who knows? Maybe your success in restoring God's world depends on your giving Tzedakah willingly.

Of course, just as workers may get their hands dirty in

doing their jobs, so must the Jews dirty their hands. In this way, Luria explained the suffering of the Jews.

But Luria did not limit the benefits of Tikkun to the Jews. Workers who rebuild a house benefit from completing the job successfully—they get paid. But the people who move into the rebuilt house benefit at least as much as the worker does. In the same way, according to Luria, if we succeed in our job of Tikkun, not only the Jews but also the rest of the world will benefit.

THINK ABOUT IT

1. According to Luria, who is responsible for Tikkun? Who will benefit from Tikkun?

2. In what sense is every Mitzvah an act of repair?

3. Imagine that you are living in Spain in 1492. Your ancestors were among the earliest Jews living in Spain, your father is a general in the Spanish army, and your family feels very much part of Spanish life. Suddenly, you and all other Jews are forced to choose between converting to Christianity or leaving Spain. In this time of Jewish suffering, would you be at all consoled by an explanation like Luria's? Discuss.

WHAT'S YOUR OPINION?

A rabbi who lived more than 200 years after Isaac Luria expressed a similar idea. Rabbi Baruch of Mezbizh said, "Every person has the vocation of making perfect something in this world. The world has need of every single human being."

תְּשׁוּבָה

TESHUVAH

tə • shōō • vä′

Teshuvah is usually translated into English as "repentance." The Hebrew word actually means "return" or "answer." A person who makes Teshuvah turns away from a bad way of life and turns toward God.

We greet Rosh HaShanah with confidence and joy because we believe God welcomes Teshuvah.

CHAPTER TWENTY

On the Luaḥ (לוּחַ), or Jewish calendar, the first ten days of the month of Tishri, extending from Rosh HaShanah through Yom Kippur, are given two Hebrew names. You already know that these High Holy Days are called Yamim Noraim (יָמִים נוֹרָאִים). This period is also called the Ten Days of Repentance, עֲשֶׂרֶת יְמֵי תְּשׁוּבָה .

The ten days from Rosh HaShanah through Yom Kippur are considered an especially fitting time for Jews to make Teshuvah. According to a Midrash, God said to Israel, "If you remake yourselves through Teshuvah during the ten days between Rosh HaShanah and Yom Kippur, on Yom Kippur I will consider you as innocent as a newborn baby."

The first ten days of Tishri are by no means the only time during the year when a Jew can make Teshuvah. We can make up our minds to change our behavior at any moment of any day of the year.

In this chapter, you will learn how belief in Teshuvah makes Judaism a hopeful religion. The stories in the second section teach that God is always eager for people to make Teshuvah. The chapter concludes with two tales that show how to start making Teshuvah.

CHAPTER SUMMARY

Lesson 1: The idea of Teshuvah makes Judaism a hopeful religion.

Lesson 2: Teshuvah is one of the most important values in Jewish life.

Lesson 3: According to tradition, the Mashiaḥ will come when all people make Teshuvah.

◁

God insisted that Jonah warn the Ninevites so they could turn away from evil and make Teshuvah.

Teshuvah and the Jewish outlook on life

Have you ever done something that left you feeling completely bad or worthless? How did you manage to shake yourself out of that feeling? If that mood ever strikes you again, knowing a little bit about the idea of Teshuvah may help restore your confidence that you are a good person. According to one Midrash, God created Teshuvah even before He created the universe. In other words, even before He made people, God made sure they would be able to change their way of life.

Many Midrashim show how belief in the possibility of Teshuvah has made Judaism a religion of hope for the future. As you read some of these Midrashim, try to answer the following questions:

(a) *What do the story of King Manasseh and the story of the Ninevites teach about Teshuvah?*
(b) *Which Rosh HaShanah traditions show that the idea of Teshuvah makes Jews hope for the best?*

FAMOUS BAALEI TESHUVAH

People who make Teshuvah are called Baalei Teshuvah (בַּעֲלֵי תְשׁוּבָה). Stories about different Baalei Teshuvah make clear the Jewish belief that people can always overcome a sinful past.

SEE FOR YOURSELF

The evil deeds of Manasseh, king of Judah, are described in 2 Kings 21:1–21. 2 Chronicles 33:12–16 records how Manasseh made Teshuvah and was restored to his throne. You can read how the Ninevites made Teshuvah in Jonah 3:5–10.

The call of the shofar at Rosh HaShanah tells us that Judgment Day has come.

In the dim light of a Leningrad synagogue, Soviet Jews read the Torah on Yom Kippur.

According to the Bible, one of the most wicked people in all Jewish history was Manasseh, king of Judah, who ruled during the seventh century B.C.E. He worshipped idols and even set them up in the Temple. Manasseh murdered many innocent people and led many others to do evil.

You might think God could never forgive such a sinful man. But the rabbis of the Talmud and Midrash knew otherwise. They pointed out that Manasseh made Teshuvah in the last years of his life. As a result, God brought him back from exile in Babylon and restored him to the throne. Manasseh removed the idols from the Temple and commanded his people to worship God.

The Bible also teaches us about a whole group of people who made Teshuvah. The people of Nineveh were not Jewish. All the same, God sent the Hebrew prophet Jonah to urge them to turn away from their wicked ways. You probably know that when Jonah tried to run away on a sailing ship, God sent a big fish to swallow him up. God was so intent on giving the people of Nineveh the chance to make Teshuvah that He refused to allow Jonah to abandon the mission.

In order to make Teshuvah, the king of Nineveh had his people fast and wear mourners' clothing. But according to the rabbis of the Talmud, this is not why God forgave them. The story in the Bible does not say that God forgave the Ninevites because He saw their mourners' clothes and fasts. It says instead that God forgave them because they had turned away from evil deeds and had begun to treat each other justly.

ROSH HASHANAH AND TESHUVAH

Another name for Rosh HaShanah is "Day of Judgment," יוֹם הַדִּין. We all stand before God the Judge, hoping for a merciful judgment.

If you had to face a judge in court and weren't sure what the verdict would be, how would you behave? You would probably dress in somber clothes. You might be afraid of appearing overconfident if you wore your very best outfit. Your appetite would surely suffer. You would be too nervous to feel like eating.

But on Rosh HaShanah, when God judges our behavior, how do we act? Because Jews believe God welcomes our Teshuvah, Rosh HaShanah is a festive occasion. We feast on apples and honey, honey cake, and other holiday foods. We also dress in holiday clothes. The rabbis of the Talmud taught that we should be confident on the Yamim Noraim. The reason for our confidence is our belief that God wants us to make Teshuvah and will forgive our misdeeds.

THINK ABOUT IT

1. What is a Baal Teshuvah?

2. Tell two stories that show how belief in Teshuvah makes Judaism a hopeful religion.

3. Imagine that you are a criminal. What do you think might keep you from becoming a Baal Teshuvah? What do you think might lead you to improve your behavior?

The Midrash says: "The gates of prayer are sometimes open, sometimes closed, but the gates of Teshuvah are forever open."

God values Teshuvah

Once upon a time, there was a prince who traveled away from home. It would take him fully one hundred days to return to his father's kingdom. He longed to see his father once again, but he didn't feel he had the strength to undertake the journey. One day, a note came from his father: "Dearest child, come back as far as your strength allows. I will go the rest of the way to meet you."

The king was willing to meet his child halfway in order to see him again. In the same way, according to the Midrash, God says to us, "Return to Me, and I will return to you." Jewish tradition stresses that because God values Teshuvah so highly, He is willing to meet each Baal Teshuvah halfway. Read how a famous rabbi learned this lesson, and ask yourself:

How did Rabbi Meir learn that God values Teshuvah?

BERURIAH'S LESSON ABOUT TESHUVAH

Is crime a threat in your neighborhood? Are there certain blocks you try to avoid? We tend to think of crime as a twentieth-century problem, but it was a problem in the days of the Talmud as well. A gang of robbers in Rabbi Meir's neighborhood made him their victim time and again.

After he had had his money stolen for what seemed like the thousandth time, Rabbi Meir came home in a rage. He said to his wife Beruriah, "I wish to God those robbers would drop dead."

Beruriah was shocked at her husband. "Have you forgotten what the prophet Ezekiel said? God doesn't want wicked people to die—He wants them to make Teshuvah and live. Instead of praying for the robbers to drop dead, why don't you pray for them to become Baalei Teshuvah?"

According to the Talmud, Beruriah's words affected Rabbi Meir deeply. He prayed for the robbers to make Teshuvah. And—what's more—they did.

SEE FOR YOURSELF

Beruriah's reminder to her husband about the importance of Teshuvah is based on Ezekiel 18:23. Can you think of another reason why it was wrong for Rabbi Meir to wish the robbers would drop dead? For a clue, review the chapter on Tefillah, especially page 128.

THINK ABOUT IT

1. What is the connection between returning and repenting?

2. Is Beruriah's lesson about Teshuvah a meaningful one in today's society? What do you think should be done to lawbreakers who are caught and convicted?

How to start making Teshuvah

A man once told Rabbi Israel of Rizhin that he wanted very much to make Teshuvah. The only problem, the man said, was that he didn't know how to go about it. The rabbi asked him if he had known how to sin. The man assured the rabbi that part had been easy: he knew he had done something wrong as soon as he had sinned. "It will be the same way with Teshuvah," the rabbi said. "Start by making Teshuvah now. As soon as you've done it, you'll know." As you read another tale about a rabbi and Teshuvah, ask yourself:

Where is the right place to begin making Teshuvah?

TESHUVAH AND THE MASHIAH

The Rabbi of Nikolsburg told the following story about himself.

"The Talmud says that if everyone in the world makes Teshuvah, the Mashiah will come. So, I asked myself, what can I do to hasten the arrival of the Mashiah? The answer was obvious. All I had to do was get everyone in the world to make Teshuvah. There was no doubt in my mind that I could do it. The only question was where to begin.

"The world is a very big place, after all. So I decided to start with the country I knew best—my own. But my own country is also very big, so I decided to start with my town. But my town is also quite large—better, I thought, to start with my own street. No, also too large. How about the members of my family? That still seemed too many. Finally, I decided to start with the only place I really knew well—myself. And even that is proving to be a lifetime job."

THINK ABOUT IT

1. Is not knowing how to improve yourself a good reason for sticking to old, unproductive habits? Explain.

2. What is another way of saying that if everyone made Teshuvah, the Mashiah would come?

GLOSSARY

in English alphabetical order

Amidah (עֲמִידָה),   literally, "standing"; the central prayer of every service, in which we address God both as "our God" and "God of our fathers [or ancestors]." The Amidah is nearly always said while standing. See also **Avot.**

Avot (אָבוֹת),   literally, "fathers." 1. Ancestors. 2. The opening blessing of the **Amidah.**

Baal Teshuvah (בַּעַל תְּשׁוּבָה),   *pl.* **Baalei Teshuvah** (בַּעֲלֵי תְּשׁוּבָה);   someone who makes **Teshuvah;** a penitent.

Bal Tashhit (בַּל תַּשְׁחִית),   literally, "do not destroy"; the idea that we are caretakers of God's world and must conserve the natural environment.

Bar Mitzvah (בַּר מִצְוָה)   and **Bat Mitzvah**   (בַּת מִצְוָה),   literally, "man of obligation" and "woman of obligation." 1. The stage of Jewish life at which a young person (usually a thirteen-year-old boy or a twelve- or thirteen-year-old girl) becomes responsible for performing the Mitzvot. 2. The ceremony that marks the beginning of this stage. 3. A boy or girl who has reached Bar or Bat Mitzvah age.

Bet Knesset (בֵּית כְּנֶסֶת),   literally, "meeting house"; a synagogue, especially in its role as a house of prayer.

Birchot HaMitzvot (בִּרְכוֹת הַמִּצְוֹת),   the **Brachot** said when performing **Mitzvot.**

Boray et HaKol (בּוֹרֵא אֶת הַכֹּל),   literally, "Creator of all things"; God as the Creator of the world.

Brachot (בְּרָכוֹת),   *sing.* **Brachah** (בְּרָכָה),   blessings. Three types of Brachot said in the home are those concerned with performing a **Mitzvah,** enjoying food and drink, and experiencing different events in our private lives. See also **She-Heheyanu.**

Brit (בְּרִית). . 1. A covenant or agreement, especially one between God and humanity. 2. The ceremony that welcomes a baby as a member of the Jewish people. See also **Brit Milah.**

Brit Milah (בְּרִית מִילָה), literally, "covenant of circumcision"; the operation performed on an eight-day-old boy as part of the ceremony that welcomes him to membership in the Jewish people.

Emet (אֱמֶת), truth.

Emunah (אֱמוּנָה), faith, belief, or trust in God.

Eretz Yisrael (אֶרֶץ יִשְׂרָאֵל), the land of Israel.

Havdalah (הַבְדָּלָה), literally, "separation"; the ceremony that marks the end of **Shabbat.**

Kabbalat Shabbat (קַבָּלַת שַׁבָּת), literally, "receiving Shabbat"; the opening service on Friday evening, consisting of six psalms and the hymn L'cha Dodi.

Kaddish (קַדִּישׁ), literally, "making holy"; a prayer said in memory of the dead.

Kadosh (קָדוֹשׁ). 1. Holy. 2. Set apart or distinctive.

Kavanah (כַּוָּנָה), literally, "intention" or "concentration"; the ability to act—and especially to pray—with true feeling and understanding.

Kedushah (קְדֻשָּׁה). 1. Holiness. 2. The name of a prayer recited during the **Amidah.**

Kiddush (קִדּוּשׁ), literally, "holiness"; a prayer over wine on Shabbat and festivals.

Kiddush HaShem (קִדּוּשׁ הַשֵּׁם), literally, "making God's name sacred." 1. Any act that brings honor to the Jewish people by causing a non-Jew to bless God's name. 2. Dying to avoid bringing disgrace to the Jewish people or dishonor to God's name; martyrdom.

Kiddushin (קִדּוּשִׁין). 1. The first part of the wedding ceremony. 2. A book of the Talmud that deals with marriage laws.

Luaḥ (לוּחַ), the Jewish calendar.

Mashiaḥ (מָשִׁיחַ), literally, "anointed one." 1. The Messiah; a savior who will reestablish the kingdom of Israel and bring a time of peace and plenty for all the world. 2. In the Bible, someone who has been anointed with holy oil, such as a king or high priest. See **Yemot HaMashiaḥ.**

Maḥzor (מַחֲזוֹר), literally, "cycle"; the festival prayerbook, including the special prayers for the **Yamim Noraim.**

Midat HaDin (מִדַּת הַדִּין), God's quality of strict justice.

Midat HaRaḥamim (מִדַּת הָרַחֲמִים), God's quality of mercy.

Midrash (מִדְרָשׁ), literally, "investigation"; a type of rabbinic literature that explains and amplifies the Bible, often through maxims and stories.

Mitzvah (מִצְוָה), *pl.* **Mitzvot** (מִצְוֹת), literally, "commandment." 1. Any action required by the Torah. 2. Any good deed or act of kindness.

Neshamah (נְשָׁמָה), soul.

Niggun (נִגּוּן), *pl.* **Niggunim** (נִגּוּנִים), a melody to which a prayer may be sung.

Olam HaBa (עוֹלָם הַבָּא). 1. The world to come. 2. Life after death.

Olam HaZeh (עוֹלָם הַזֶּה). 1. This world. 2. Our present life on earth.

Pesaḥ (פֶּסַח), Passover, the first of the **Shalosh Regalim.**

Shabbat (שַׁבָּת), from the Hebrew word meaning "to rest"; the Sabbath day.

Shalosh Regalim (שָׁלֹשׁ רְגָלִים), three festivals—Pesaḥ, Shavuot, and Sukkot—which in ancient times required a pilgrimage to the Temple in Jerusalem.

Shavuot (שָׁבוּעוֹת), literally, "weeks"; the second of the **Shalosh Regalim.** Shavuot is also called Ḥag HaKatzir (חַג הַקָּצִיר), or "harvest holiday"; Ḥag HaBikkurim (חַג הַבִּכּוּרִים), or "holiday of first fruits"; and Zman Matan Torateinu (זְמַן מַתַּן תּוֹרָתֵנוּ), or "time of the giving of the Torah."

SheHeḥeyanu (שֶׁהֶחֱיָנוּ), the **Brachah** that expresses our thanks to God for the good things we experience in life.

Sheker (שֶׁקֶר), falsehood.

Shema (שְׁמַע), literally, "hear." 1. A short way of referring to the six words that mean "Hear, O Israel, the Lord is our God, the Lord is One." 2. The three-paragraph prayer that begins with "Hear, O Israel" and includes the **V'Ahavta.**

Shulḥan Aruch (שֻׁלְחָן עָרוּךְ), literally, "prepared table"; a guide to Jewish law and practice compiled in the sixteenth century by Joseph Caro.

Siddur (סִדּוּר), *pl.* Siddurim (סִדּוּרִים), the Jewish prayerbook.

Sukkot (סֻכּוֹת), literally, "booths"; the third of the **Shalosh Regalim.**

Talmud (תַּלְמוּד), literally, "learning" or "instruction"; sacred books of Jewish practice compiled about 1500 years ago. The Jerusalem (or Palestinian) Talmud contains the discussions of the rabbis in the academies of Israel; the Babylonian Talmud contains the discussions of the rabbis of the academies in Babylonia.

Tefillah (תְּפִלָה). 1. Prayer in general. 2. The **Amidah.**

Teshuvah (תְּשׁוּבָה), literally, "return" or "answer"; repentance. See also **Baal Teshuvah.**

Tikkun (תִּקּוּן), repair or improvement. The idea of Tikkun suggests that we are God's partners in improving the world.

V'Ahavta (וְאָהַבְתָּ), literally, "and you shall love"; the paragraph of the **Shema** that includes the **Mitzvot** of loving God, teaching God's words to our children, reciting the Shema at night and in the morning, wearing Tefillin, and putting a Mezuzah on the doorpost.

Yamim Noraim (יָמִים נוֹרָאִים), literally, "Days of Awe"; the ten days beginning with Rosh HaShanah and ending with Yom Kippur. The Yamim Noraim are also known as the Ten Days of Repentance (עֲשֶׂרֶת יְמֵי תְּשׁוּבָה).

Yemot HaMashiaḥ (יְמוֹת הַמָּשִׁיחַ), literally, "days of the Mashiaḥ"; a future age of peace and perfection. See also **Mashiaḥ.**

INDEX